1. In the opening lyrics of ABBA's 'Super Trouper', the super trouper beams are going to do what?

2. In verse 1 of Ottawan's 'D.I.S.C.O', what does 'S' stand for?

3. Blondie came 6th in the UK charts of 1983, but how many UK number 1's have they had all-together?

4. In what decade did The Detroit Spinners form?

5. How many Christmas albums has Kenny Rogers recorded altogether?

Some of the most iconic shows from the 80s are still fresh in our memories! From action-packed shows like the A-Team and Knight Rider, through to comedy classics like Only Fools and Horses and Blackadder, you could be sure your TV was tuned into a masterpiece!

Many channels still show replays of 80s shows. Only Fools and Horses, for example, have 64 episodes that are often played on repeat today – It's a wonder you aren't quoting them word for word by now!

And even if Del Boy didn't predict correctly and you never cashed in on your millions, if you had a TV back in the 80s, then you truly were blessed - with supreme shows like Desmond's, Yes Minister, and Hi-de-Hi!

1. Which year was Blackadder first aired?

2. What is the name of Del Boy and Rodney's uncle in Only Fools and Horses?

3. What was Desmond's last name in Desmond's?

4. Who played Michael Knight in Knight Rider?

5. How many members are there in the A-Team?

1. 1983 2. Uncle Albert 3. Ambrose 4. David Hasselhoff 5. 4

The 80s was a haven for live music goers. Concerts and music festivals were enhancing, and with more travel opportunities, came more international festivals.

Some festivals were just for fun, but some had a deeper meaning behind them. Live Aid for example, was a benefit concert with an aim to fundraise for a good cause.

Held on 13th July, 1985, Live Aid was organised by Bob Geldof and Midge Ure, to help raise funds which would then help relieve famine in Ethiopia. Raising approximately £150 million, famous artists including Queen, Boomtown Rats, Elvis Costello and Duran Duran donned the stage to raise!

Other festivals in the 80s included the 1980 Heatwave (Bowmanville, Ontario), 1983 US Festival (Devore, California), and the iconic and much loved 1985 Rock in Rio – which had fantastic headlining acts including Iron Maiden, Queen, Rod Stewart and Ozzy Osborne!

1. How many people attended the 10-day-long Rock in Rio in 1985?

2. What is Elvis Costello's birth name?

3. Rod Stewart made his way through the 80s as a common musician, but what year did he eventually get knighted?

4. Which day of the week did the Boomtown Rats sing about not liking?

1. Around 1.4 million people 2. Declan Patrick MacManus 3. 2016 4. Mondays

In 1965, seatbelts were declared a mandatory addition to all new cars in the UK, but there was no law in place stating they must be worn. Throughout the 70s, the UK government tried time and time again to make wearing seatbelts a legal requirement, but it was only put into effect in 1983.

In 1983, the fine for not wearing your seatbelt was £50, but in current times, you could be landed with a fine of up to £500!

True or False:

1. In the 1980s, theory tests weren't a thing.

2. You didn't need a driving license in the 80s.

3. Provisional licenses were extended until the age of 70 in 1982.

4. In the 80s, you still had to demonstrate arm signals in driving tests.

5. Three wheelers were the most popular car in the 1980s.

1. True 2. False 3. True 4. False 5. False

1. The 1980 Olympic Games were held where?

2. In what year was the Berlin Wall pulled down?

3. Which space shuttle tragically exploded in 1986?

4. Which 1980 musical was originally sung in French, but was eventually translated into English?

5. How long did Erno Rubik (Rubik's Cube inventor), take to solve the cube?

1. Moscow, Russia 2. 1989 3. Challenger 4. Les Miserables 5. 4 weeks

The third generation of Nintendo's game consoles began in 1983, with the release of the NES! Only two other Nintendo consoles came before, The 1972 'Brown Box', and the 'Colour TV Game' series (which was released in 1977 and only had one game per console).

The Nintendo Entertainment System (NES) featured interchangeable cartridges, bringing a new lease of life to the gaming world.

Some well-known games began with the NES, such as The Legend of Zelda and Super Mario Bros., who released 12 launch games and then later developed more games to accompany the console.

Test your 80s gaming knowledge!

1. Other than Grey, The Legend of Zelda came with what other coloured cartridges when they were released for the NES?

2. How many NES copies of Super Mario Bros. did Nintendo sell?

3. Including the D-pad, how many buttons does the original NES controller have?

4. What was another name for the NES?

1. Gold 2. 40 million 3. 8 4. Famicom

Stay in the '80s
I carried a watermelon
8bit
8bit
select start
TURBO
WALL ST
8bit
select start
TURBO

Human League took over Christmas with their chart-topping hit 'Don't You Want Me'. Holding number one for five whole weeks, this song was also the best-selling song of the year, with approximately 1.15 million sales! – It seems people really did want it!

The top 10 for 1981 in the UK was:

1. DON'T YOU WANT ME - HUMAN LEAGUE
2. TAINTED LOVE - SOFT CELL
3. STAND & DELIVER - ADAM & THE ANTS
4. PRINCE CHARMING - ADAM & THE ANTS
5. THIS OLE HOUSE - SHAKIN' STEVENS
6. VIENNA - ULTRAVOX
7. ONE DAY IN YOUR LIFE - MICHAEL JACKSON
8. MAKING YOUR MIND UP - BUCKS FIZZ
9. SHADDUP YOU FACE - JOE DOLCE MUSIC THEATRE
10. BIRDIE SONG - TWEETS

1. Adam and the Ants have made it twice on the top 10 list, but how many number 1's have they had overall?

2. Michael Jackson sadly passed away in 2009, but in which year was he born?

3. The Tweets 'Birdie Song' only has two letters of the alphabet in its lyrics. Which two letters are they?

4. What is Shakin' Stevens' real birth name?

5. The English duo Softcell consists of who?

1. 2 2. 1958 3. D, A 4. Michael Barratt 5. Marc Almond and David Ball

Tri-colour Pasta

From the decade that brought a new age of yummy meals and creative treats, it's no surprise that adding colour to meals was the 80s way to go! Who wants beige pasta when you could jazz it up with red and green?

Ingredients:

Tri-colour rotini pasta - 3 cups full before cooking

Water - as needed

1/2 teaspoon + a pinch of salt

1/4 cup of butter

2 large basil leaves - finely chopped

1/4 cup grated parmesan cheese

4 cloves of garlic - finely chopped

1 tablespoon of red chilli flakes

1/4 teaspoon of lemon zest

2 tablespoons of lemon juice

Method:

Bring a pan of water to boil and add ½ teaspoon of salt. Add the pasta to the water and cook for around 8 minutes. Then drain off the water and keep the pasta to one side.

Heat a frying pan and add the butter, garlic and red chilli flakes together. Fry for around 2 minutes until the butter is melted and garlic is mixed wholly.

Add in 2 tablespoons of lemon juice and a pinch of salt and allow another quick stir. Cook this for another 2 to 3 minutes until the sauce boils.

Pop your colourful pasta into the sauce and mix and toss well until the sauce coats the pasta.

Add the chopped basil leaves, lemon zest and parmesan cheese and mix well.

Time to eat your well-deserved 80s dish!

Name: Mel Gibson (Mel Columcille Gerard Gibson)
Born: January 3rd, 1956
Occupations: Actor, film director, producer, screenwriter
Most Famous 80s Appearance: Lethal Weapon

Mel Gibson is well known for his 80s roles in Gallipoli, Lethal Weapon, Mad Max (2), and Tequila Sunrise, though it wasn't until the 90s when he began directing and producing other movies. Gibson was born in New York, and is of Irish descent – not bad to say he played as a Scottish warrior!

True or false:

1. Mel Gibson has previously been roommates with actor Geoffrey Rush.

2. Mel Gibson revealed that he has a "bulbous kidney" - a condition where two kidneys fuse into one.

3. Gibson has five siblings.

4. Mel Gibson made only $400 for his first role in a film.

5. Gibson was named after an Irish saint.

"You'll never find peace of mind until you listen to your heart."
– George Michael

On 8th December 1980, John Lennon (co-leader of The Beatles), was fatally shot outside his New York residence, the Dakota.

John and Ono Lennon were on their way into their apartment from a recording session when John was shot five times in the back by Mark David Chapman, a fan of The Beatles. Just hours before, when they had left the apartment, The Lennons were approached by Chapman, who had asked for John's autograph.

After he had parted with his gun, Chapman waited for the police to arrive with no sign of putting up a struggle, and went willingly with the police.

Chapman's motive was unusual and he had allegedly planned out John Lennon's murder three months prior. Being a long-time fan of The Beatles, Chapman had turned against John Lennon after Lennon claimed that the Beatles were "More popular than Jesus." – It is also said that Chapman grew jealous of the way the star had been living.

Were you a Beatlemaniac? Take this quiz to find out!

1. What was the last song John Lennon ever played for a paying audience?

2. Who was The Beatles original drummer?

3. How many children does John Lennon have?

4. What was the name of The Beatles' first single?

5. Which song has the lyrics "All the lonely people, where do they all belong"?

1. I Saw Her Standing There 2. Pete Best 3. 2 (Sean and Julian) 4. Love Me Do 5. Eleanor Rigby

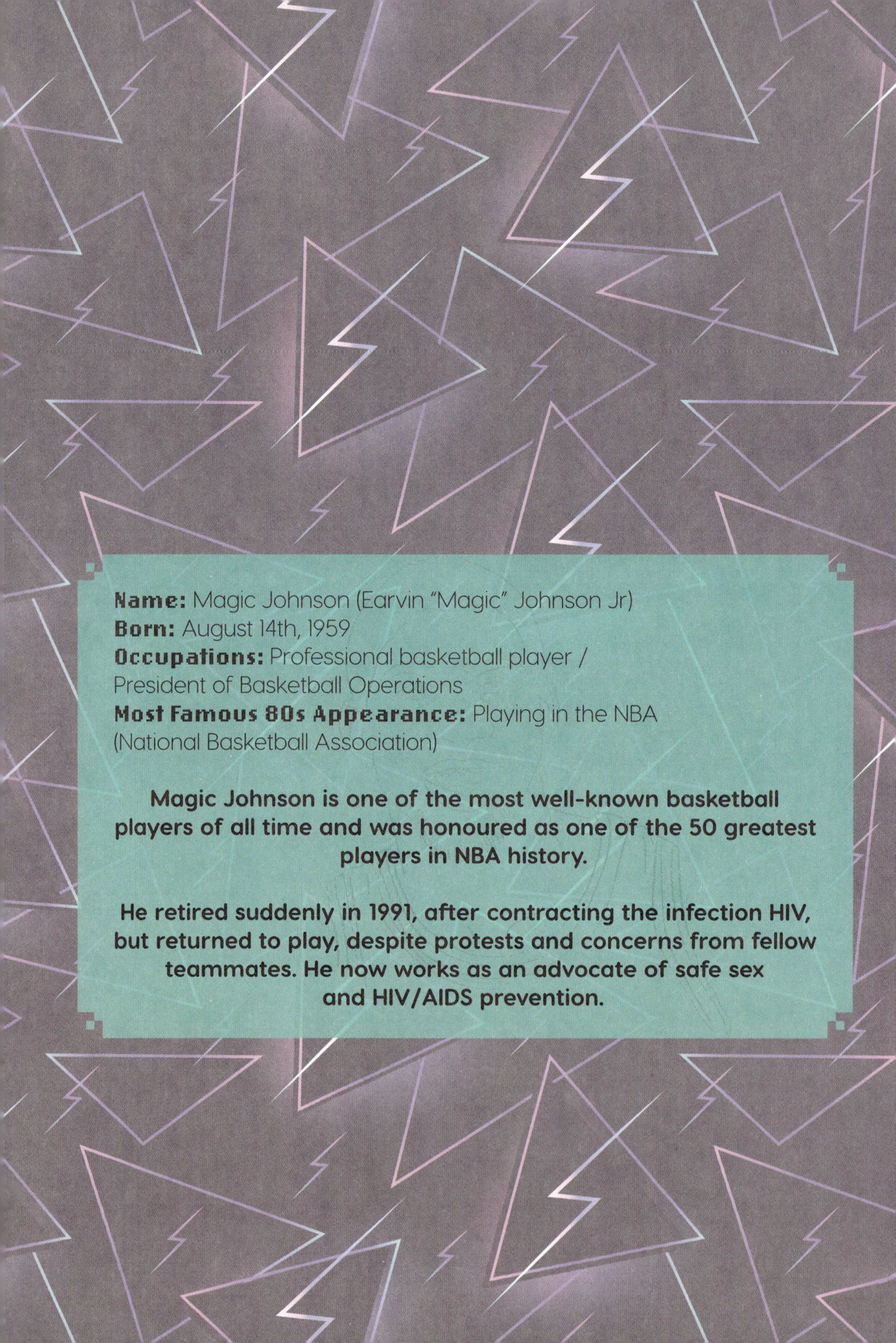

Name: Magic Johnson (Earvin "Magic" Johnson Jr)
Born: August 14th, 1959
Occupations: Professional basketball player / President of Basketball Operations
Most Famous 80s Appearance: Playing in the NBA (National Basketball Association)

Magic Johnson is one of the most well-known basketball players of all time and was honoured as one of the 50 greatest players in NBA history.

He retired suddenly in 1991, after contracting the infection HIV, but returned to play, despite protests and concerns from fellow teammates. He now works as an advocate of safe sex and HIV/AIDS prevention.

True or false:

1. Johnson is seven foot tall.

2. Johnson played for the Los Angeles Lakers.

3. Magic Johnson coached the Phoenix Suns.

4. He is nicknamed 'Magic' because of his love for magicians.

5. He is the CEO of Magic Johnson Enterprises.

1. False – He is six-nine 2. True 3. False – He coached Los Angeles Lakers 4. False 5. True

In 1982, Dexy's Midnight Runners took the world by storm with Come On Eileen. Spending four weeks at number one, with an estimated 1.21 million sales, this song is still popular on pub jukeboxes and milestone birthday parties to this day!

The top 10 for 1982 in the UK was:

1. COME ON EILEEN - DEXY'S MIDNIGHT RUNNERS
2. FAME - IRENE CARA
3. EYE OF THE TIGER - SURVIVOR
4. THE LIONS SLEEPS TONIGHT - TIGHT FIT
5. DO YOU REALLY WANT TO HURT ME - CULTURE CLUB
6. PASS THE DUTCHIE - MUSICAL YOUTH
7. I DON'T WANNA DANCE - EDDY GRANT
8. SEVEN TEARS - GOOMBAY DANCE BAND
9. EBONY AND IVORY - PAUL MCCARTNEY WITH STEVIE WONDER
10. TOWN CALLED MALICE/PRECIOUS - JAM

1. Dexy's Midnight Runners had another chart-topper two years earlier in 1980, but which song was it?

2. Which iconic 1982 movie was Survivor's 'Eye of the Tiger' the theme tune to?

3. In The Jam's 'Town Called Malice' lyrics, what does the whole street believe in?

4. The South African Broadcasting Corporation banned Paul McCartney and Stevie Wonder's 'Ebony and Ivory' song, after Wonder dedicated it to whom?

5. Culture Club originally had four members; Boy George, Mikey Craig, Roy Hay and which other artist?

1. Geno 2. Rocky 3 3. Sunday's roast beef 4. Nelson Mandela 5. Jon Moss

Reeboks, Converse, Doc Martens... the time of unisex shoes was thrown upon us in the 1980s. Sportswear was at an all-time high, and even little girls in dresses wanted to don their outfits with some lace up boots or trainers.

These shoes have been around much longer than the 80s, but it was only the 80s when they really became the shoe of the decade.

If you scuffed your converse, you'd be sure to get chased around the house by your mum – but if you scuffed your docs, then congratulations! Those shoes are made to last!

In fact, we're sure many 80s kids will still own a pair today (am I wrong?).

Test your sole knowledge with these quick questions:

1. Though only becoming popular in 1979, when did Reebok actually launch?

2. What was the brand Doc Martens called before they gained that name?

3. Which sport was Converse All Star first created for?

1. 1958 2. Griggs 3. Basketball

A favourite of children around the world, everybody remembers the iconic ponies that shaped the toy industry. But did you know that the My Little Pony gang had a predecessor? My 'Pretty' Pony was introduced by Hasbro in 1981, one year before the 'little' ponies stole the spotlight. If you have some older ponies stored away in your attic, it might be worth dusting them off, as collectors will buy them for a nice price.

Do you know your facts about My Little Pony? Let's find out!

1. In 1983, a range of My Little Ponies helped to add a splash of fun into bath time, what were they called?

2. Candy Cane ponies were first released in 1988. But what was special about them?

3. Hasbro released a set of male ponies in 1986, what were the set called?

4. Where does Applejack live?

5. What 'cutie mark' did Firefly have on her back leg?

1. Sea Ponies 2. They had scents that matched their names 3. Adventure Boy Ponies 4. Sweet Apple Acres 5. Two lightning bolts

The 1980s had the best holidays for families who were lucky enough to get on a plane and explore the world.

Getting down-under in Australia, trailing the sandy beaches of the Caribbean or wrapping up warm in Antarctica, not the most common places of today, but back then these were the places to be!

It seems people in the 80s craved to go out of their comfort zone and explore territory they'd never stepped on before – and let's face it, who wouldn't want to dip their toes in an exotic ocean or pose with a polarbear?

What was your favourite holiday you went on in the 80s?

Travel Trivia!

1. Which country has the strange phenomenon site 'Blood Falls'?

2. How many countries use the Eastern Caribbean Dollar?

3. Which country has the world's longest stretch of straight railway?

1. Antarctica 2. 8 3. Australia

The 1980s had a whole decade of wacky hairdos, crazy TV shows and world-changing events.

How much can you remember from this colourful decade?

1. Which video game was the most popular game of the 80s?

2. Which song plays during both the opening and closing credits of 'The Breakfast Club'?

3. Whitney Houston won how many Grammy Awards throughout the 1980s?

4. Who Played Duckie Dale in 'Pretty in Pink'?

5. Which shoe brand did Run DMC make popular by including them in the music video to "Walk This Way"?

1. Super Mario Bros. 2. Don't You (Forget About Me) – Simple Minds 3. Two 4. Jon Cryer 5. Adidas

Being a child of the 80s, you've probably seen the famous movie 'The Titanic'. This was based on a true event, which was brought back into the spotlight in 1985 - a whole seventy three years after the sinking.

The RMS Titanic passenger ship sank in 1912, and efforts were made to locate this shipwreck immediately after, but limitations in tech at the time stopped searchers being successful.

Former Navy officer Robert D. Ballard led his first expedition for the search of this mysterious shipwreck in 1977, but again the search was unsuccessful.

He teamed up with French Oceanographer Jean-Louis Michel in 1985, where they used a submersible to search the ocean floor, eventually passing over a huge boiler – belonging to the RMS Titanic!

The rest of the ship was found nearby the following day – debris scattering as far as 2 miles around the ship. After exploring the wreck using submersibles, new information came to light about the unforgettable 1912 sinking of this grand passenger ship.

Is Titanic your go-to movie?
Can you guess these answers correctly?

1. How long did the Titanic take to build?

2. How many Academy Awards did the movie Titanic win?

3. In which month did the RMS Titanic sink?

4. Which ship was first to the scene of the sinking in 1912?

5. Where was the RMS Titanic headed when it sank?

1. Three years 2. 11 3. April 4. Carpathia 5. New York City

Name: Princess Diana (Diana Frances Spencer)
Born: July 1st, 1961
Died: August 31st, 1997 (aged 36)
Occupations: Princess of Wales
Most Famous 80s Appearance: Her marriage to Charles, Prince of Wales

Diana was born into British nobility. She was close to the royals growing up, and before becoming a princess, she worked as a teaching assistant in a nursery. Diana was well known and liked throughout Britain for her involvement in campaigns for the acceptance of AIDs patients and helping the Red Cross.

True or false:

1. Princess Diana had an avid passion for all things ballet.

2. Princess Diana's sister dated Prince Charles first.

3. Princess Diana was born in Birmingham.

4. Princess Diana and Prince Charles' wedding took place at Buckingham Palace.

5. Elton John sung at Princess Diana's funeral.

1. True 2. True 3. False – Norfolk 4. False – St Paul's Cathedral 5. True

A handful of chefs in the 80s had risen to stardom (Just like a nice Victoria sponge cake), and brought full entertainment to mothers, fathers and even grandparents within this tasteful decade!

Who: Ken Hom **Year:** 1983
Show: Ken Hom's Chinese Cookery

Who: Martha Stewart **Year:** 1982
Book: Entertaining

Who: Keith Floyd **Year:** 1984
Show: Floyd on Fish

Who: Martin Yan **Year:** 1982
Show: Yan Can Cook

Think you know your TV chefs, why not test yourself!

1. Though a celebrity chef, Martha Stewart made other news later on in her career, being sent to prison for four felony charges. What year did she get sentenced?

2. Ken Hom received which award from Queen Elizabeth II in 2009?

3. How many times was Kieth Floyd married?

4. What was Martin Yan's first published book called?

1. 2004 2. An OBE 3. 4 times 4. Chinese Recipes, 1978

Culture Club owned 1983 with their hit song Karma Chameleon. Bagging 955,000 sales in this one year, this song stayed number one for six weeks running!

Though their lead in the charts had come and go, this song certainly hadn't, and is often heard on the radio today!

The top 10 for 1983 in the UK was:

1. KARMA CHAMELEON – CULTURE CLUB

2. UPTOWN GIRL – BILLY JOEL

3. RED RED WINE – UB40

4. LET'S DANCE – DAVID BOWIE

5. TOTAL ECLIPSE OF THE HEART – BONNIE TYLER

6. TRUE – SPANDAU BALLET

7. DOWN UNDER – MEN AT WORK

8. BILLIE JEAN – MICHAEL JACKSON

9. ONLY YOU – FLYING PICKETS

10. ALL NIGHT LONG (ALL NIGHT) – LIONEL RICHIE

Got what it takes to correctly answer this quiz?

1. In 'Let's Dance', what coloured shoes does Bowie mention?

2. What is Bonnie Tyler's real name?

3. How many UK number ones did Michael Jackson have?

4. Lionel Richie sung about being "Once, twice, three times a" what?

5. In Billy Joel's 'Uptown Girl', what can't he afford to buy the girl?

1. Red shoes 2. Gaynor Hopkins 3. 7 4. Lady 5. Pearls

The Highest grossing film of the 1980s was Steven Spielberg's ET, grossing a huge $663,400,925 in worldwide box office receipts! Released on the 11th June 1982, this film became an instant classic, and cemented Spielberg as a directorial force to be reckoned with!

The top 5 highest grossing films of the 1980s:
(based on their initial box-office releases)

1. E.T. the Extra -Terrestrial - 1982
2. Indiana Jones and the Last Crusade - 1989
3. Batman - 1989
4. Rain Man - 1988
5. Back to the Future Part II - 1989

Do any of these surprise you? Which film do you think is most deserving of the top spot?

1. Who played Joker in the 1989 'Batman' movie?

2. In 'Back to the Future Part II', the time machine used is a car fitted with a flux capacitor, but which car was used?

3. In 'Rain Man', Dustin Hoffman plays the lead role, but which character is it he plays?

4. In 'Indiana Jones and the Last Crusade', which castle does Indiana Jones infiltrate?

5. In 'E.T. the Extra-Terrestrial', how many siblings did Elliott have?

1. Jack Nicholson 2. DMC DeLorean 3. Raymond Babbitt 4. Castle Brunwald 5. 2 (1 younger sister and 1 older brother)

With a combination of soft nougat and milk chocolate, it's no wonder this melt-in-your-mouth snack has kept its popularity over the years. Invented all the way back in the 1920s, this snack-sized bar has really become a household name, finding its way into children's packed lunches around the world! Yes we're talking about the Milky Way!

In 1989, a bright and noisy advertisement took over TV screens around the UK. Two cartoon cars, one blue, the other red, decided to have a race…

The red car and the blue car had a race,
All that red could do was stuff his face,
He eats everything he sees,
From trucks to prickly trees,
But smart old blue he took the milky way!

He's looking for a chocolate treat,
Fluffy and light,
Cause he knows it won't spoil his app-e-tite,

mm mm MMMM!

Oh no! the bridge has gone, poor old red just can't carry on,
But smart old blue, he took the milky way!

Do you know which popular confectionary company owns the Milky Way bar? (Here's a clue, it's another chocolate bar!)

A: Mars

STAY in the '80s
4
HE SLIMED ME

Full of inventions, creativity and joy, the 80s really was the place to be. Go back in time with this trivia, and test yourself on your 80s knowledge!

1. What was the main female character in 'The Terminator' named?

2. Which video game from the 80s has the same name as a Shakespeare play?

3. In 1982 which newspapers were stored in boxes designed to look like TVs?

4. Which character was the only major male in Strawberry Shortcake and Friends?

5. Which four colours are found on the toy 'Simon'?

6. Which TV character had a brother named Derek and uncle named Albert?

7. How many actors played James Bond in the 80s?

8. The first mobile phones were introduced to the public In 1983, by who?

9. Which American sweet became popular because of E.T.?

10. What does VHS stand for?

6. Rodney Trotter 7. 3 (Roger Moore, Timothy Dalton, Sean Connery) 8. Motorola 9. Reese's Pieces 10: Video Home System

back to 80's

Some toys have a short but iconic role, and the same could be said for Hasbro's Poochie! Yes, this sweet little poodle, with its adorable ears and paws and spectacular sunglasses, only lasted a short while, but brought smiles to many 80s children. In 1984, a short movie about this little white poodle was released, sending Poochie on an adventure of a lifetime!

Some other named toys that were short-lived were BraveStarr, Teddy Ruxpin, Keypers, Zoids and the Power Glove!

Do you know your toys? Test yourself with this short quiz!

1. Where did Poochie travel to in her movie short?

2. What was Teddy Ruxpin's species?

3. Which games console was the Power Glove designed for?

4. Tonka, who produced the Keypers, are more commonly known for creating what?

5. Which country did BraveStarr originate?

1. Cairo, Egypt 2. Illiops 3. The NES 4. Toy trucks 5. America

Compared to today, the 1980s toy market was very laid back. I mean, who cares if a Jart stabs through your hand or a mini hammock caused asphyxiation? There's a reason some toys are no longer around, some were downright dangerous! Let's take a look at some memorably lethal toys of the decade!

Slip N' Slide

This popular summer activity sure knew how to make people crack up – literally... These garden water slides were dangerous for teens and adults, causing spinal injuries, broken bones and friction burns to many who wanted to feel the thrill of a slippery floor. A recommendation statement had to be brought out eventually, with a disclaimer that only children should use the slide... talk about a slippery slope!

Hang 10 Mini Hammock

Who doesn't like to chill in the garden on a hot summer's day? Well, many parents found the perfect garden product for their children with these mini hammocks. That is, until they began tangling themselves up between the ropes and fabric, causing asphyxiation – and at least 12 deaths. Dubbed the 'death cocoon', this product managed to stay on the market until 1996!

Jarts

If stabbing your hand was in your school holiday plans, then these garden darts were the perfect toy! Aimed at children, these lawn darts were lethal in so many ways. They injured around 61,000 people before their ban in 1988, after an 11 year old girl was put into a coma after receiving a head injury from one!

'Do They Know It's Christmas?' appeared like a magical Christmas present in 1984, and has haunted the radio every Christmas since! This charity single, organised by Bob Geldof and including many celebrity faces (Band Aid) had sales of over 2.4 million!

The top 10 for 1984 in the UK was:

1. DO THEY KNOW IT'S CHRISTMAS? - BAND AID
2. I JUST CALLED TO SAY I LOVE YOU - STEVIE WONDER
3. RELAX - FRANKIE GOES TO HOLLYWOOD
4. TWO TRIBES - FRANKIE GOES TO HOLLYWOOD
5. CARELESS WHISPER - GEORGE MICHAEL
6. LAST CHRISTMAS/EVERYTHING SHE WANTS - WHAM!
7. HELLO - LIONEL RICHIE
8. AGADOO - BLACK LACE
9. GHOSTBUSTERS - RAY PARKER JR
10. FREEDOM - WHAM!

1. What famous band was George Michael a member of?

2. In Black Lace's 'Agadoo', which fruit is mentioned many times in the lyrics?

3. Ghostbusters is an iconic song and also a popular film. How many members of the ghostbusters are there in the original film?

4. How many UK number ones did Wham! have?

5. What is Stevie Wonder's real name?

1. Wham! 2. Pineapple 3. 3 members 4. 5 5. Stevland Hardaway Morris

Iconic Cocktail – Tequila Sunrise

Just like the 1988 romantic crime film with old-school hunks Mel Gibson and Kurt Russel, this fruity concoction will get you in the mood for love! The tequila sunrise makes a perfect cocktail for any 80s themed discos or cocktail parties!

Ingredients:

Ice
1 large orange (or 2 small ones), juiced
½ lemon, juiced
2tsp (teaspoon) grenadine
50ml tequila
1tbsp (tablespoon) triple sec
1 cocktail cherry (for toppings)

Tools:

Your favourite 80s glass (should be tall)
A wacky cocktail stick – bonus points if it's neon!
Cocktail umbrella – you know you want to!

Method:

1. Pour the two teaspoons of grenadine into the bottom of the glass and put to one side. Using a cocktail shaker (or sealed container), shake ice, tequila, triple sec, and fruit juices all together until mixed well.

2. Add a couple of ice cubes to the glass from before, then gently strain the cocktail into it, being careful not to disturb the grenadine too much.

3. Add your finishing touches – cherry, cocktail stick, umbrella – and enjoy.

(It tastes so good it should be criminal!)

Televisions became increasingly popular in the 1980s. You could watch your favourite soaps, cartoons, the daily news and even live events. One very royal event, the wedding of Prince Charles and Lady Diana Spencer, had a mass audience, as over 28 million viewers tuned in to watch the wedding of the decade!

Though this wedding was the highest live event to be aired in the 1980s, It was actually EastEnders that took the limelight in 1986, with 30.15 million viewers tuning in to watch the Christmas special!

Top 5 most viewed TV moments in the 1980s:

1. EastEnders (1986, BBC1) 30.15m

2. Royal Wedding - Charles & Diana (1981, ITV/BBC) 28.4m

3. Coronation Street (1989, ITV) 26.9m

4. Dallas (1980, BBC1) 21.6m

5. To the Manor Born (1980, BBC1) 21.55m

"When you don't have anything, you don't have anything to lose. Right?"
–Samantha from Sixteen Candles (1984) played by Molly Ringwald

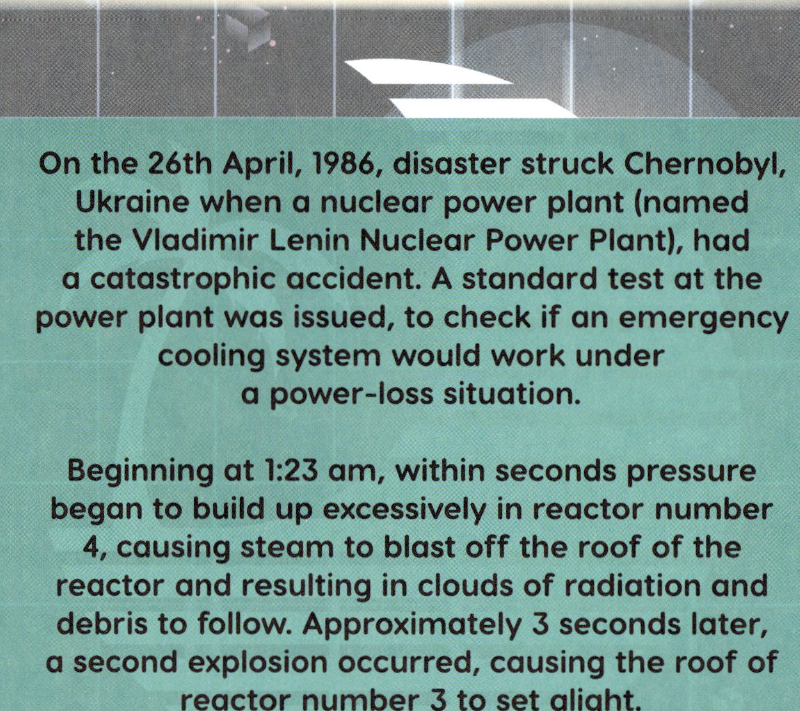

On the 26th April, 1986, disaster struck Chernobyl, Ukraine when a nuclear power plant (named the Vladimir Lenin Nuclear Power Plant), had a catastrophic accident. A standard test at the power plant was issued, to check if an emergency cooling system would work under a power-loss situation.

Beginning at 1:23 am, within seconds pressure began to build up excessively in reactor number 4, causing steam to blast off the roof of the reactor and resulting in clouds of radiation and debris to follow. Approximately 3 seconds later, a second explosion occurred, causing the roof of reactor number 3 to set alight.

Due to loss of power during the test (which was shut down purposely), no automatic systems were in place to shut down this emergency. Firefighters fought the blaze, but had no protective gear to fight against the radiation, and many were among the numbers of those killed by radiation exposure.

How good are you at geography? Test yourself with this true or false quiz!

1. Ukraine is the biggest (fully European) country in Europe.

2. Pip Ivan is the highest mountain in Ukraine.

3. The chicken Kyiv originated in Kyiv, Ukraine!

1. True! - If you take away Russia (which sits in both Europe and Asia), Ukraine is actually the largest, wholly European country!
2. False! Mount Hoverla is the tallest, at 2061m tall.
3. False – Its origins are often debated, but this tasty main dish isn't Ukrainian.

The 80s was a wild decade for fashion. Everywhere you looked, people had an entire different style and no wardrobe looked the same. But the diversity in fashion brought a demand for more clothing shops.

If you were born in the 80s, you'll probably remember being dragged around busy clothing shops with your family, being forced to hold clothes up to yourself or wait with bags upon bags of shopping until your mother found the perfect dress.

Shops such as Fosters, Chelsea Girl, Etam and Tammy Girl lined our highstreets with their fashionable double denim outfits and teal, white and purple tracksuits.

Though many 80s fashion shops have since closed down, some have survived and others have evolved. Chelsea Girl for instance, evolved into the now popular River Island.

Are you brainy and fashionable?

Try these questions to find out!

1. What shape could be found beside the name 'Chelsea Girl' on many of their shops?

2. What kind of clothing shop was Fosters?

3. Where was the first ever Etam shop based?

1. Heart 2. Male clothing 3. Berlin, Germany

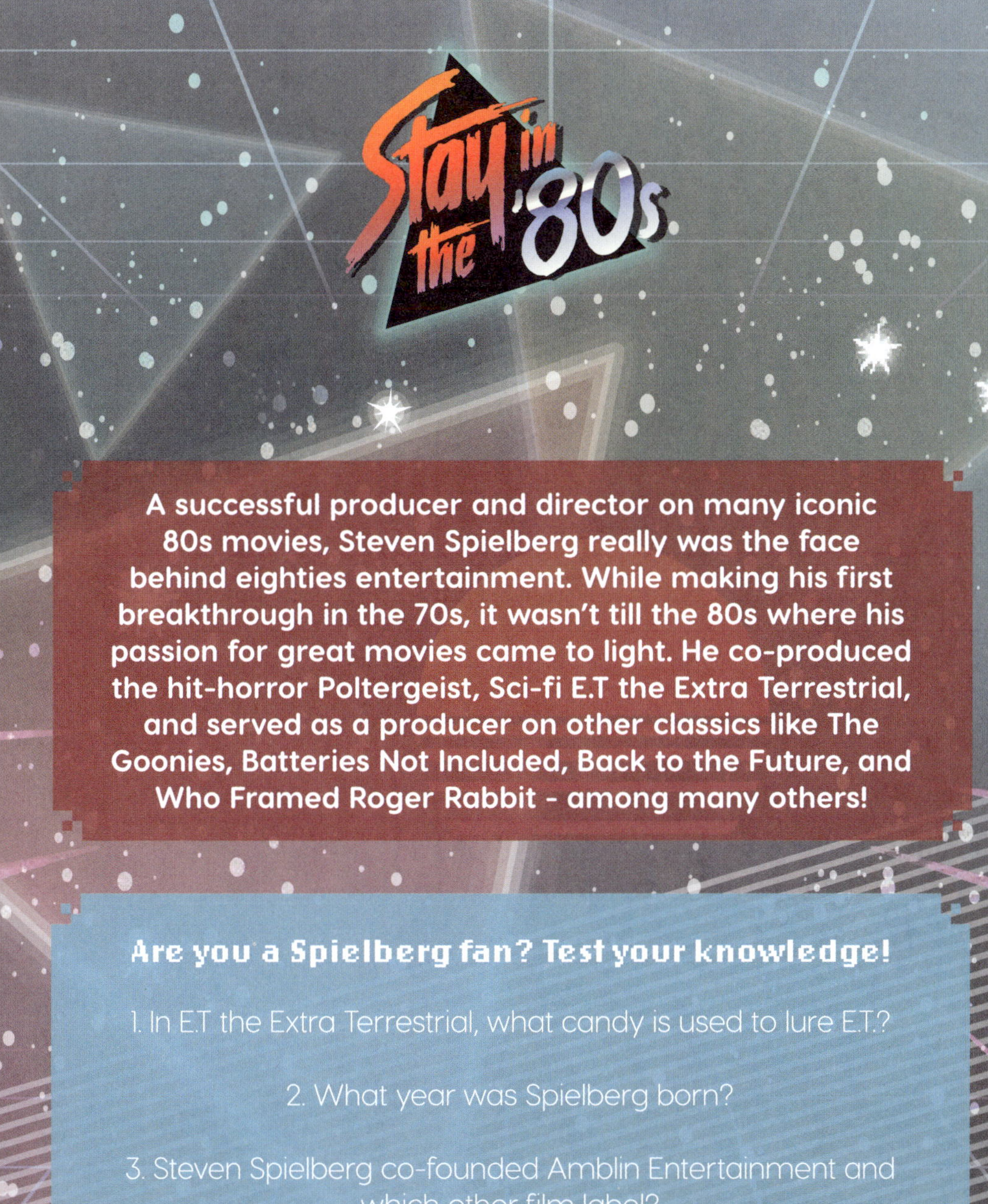

A successful producer and director on many iconic 80s movies, Steven Spielberg really was the face behind eighties entertainment. While making his first breakthrough in the 70s, it wasn't till the 80s where his passion for great movies came to light. He co-produced the hit-horror Poltergeist, Sci-fi E.T the Extra Terrestrial, and served as a producer on other classics like The Goonies, Batteries Not Included, Back to the Future, and Who Framed Roger Rabbit - among many others!

Are you a Spielberg fan? Test your knowledge!

1. In E.T the Extra Terrestrial, what candy is used to lure E.T.?

2. What year was Spielberg born?

3. Steven Spielberg co-founded Amblin Entertainment and which other film label?

1. Reese's Pieces 2. 1946 3. Dreamworks

Jennifer Rush stole the hearts of many in 1985, with her power ballad 'The Power of Love'! Taking its time to reach its peak, this song began at number 97 in June, but sky rocketed in October to first place, spending five whole weeks at number 1 and selling 1.2 million!

The top 10 for 1985 in the UK was:

1. THE POWER OF LOVE - JENNIFER RUSH

2. I KNOW HIM SO WELL - ELAINE PAIGE AND BARBARA DICKSON

3. INTO THE GROOVE - MADONNA

4. 19 - PAUL HARDCASTLE

5. FRANKIE - SISTER SLEDGE

6. DANCING IN THE STREET - DAVID BOWIE AND MICK JAGGER

7. MOVE CLOSER - PHYLLIS NELSON

8. A GOOD HEART - FEARGAL SHARKEY

9. TAKE ON ME - A-HA

10. LOVE & PRIDE - KING

Test your knowledge of the 1985 UK charts with this quiz!

1. Which war does Paul Hardcastle's song '19' reference?

2. A-Ha is made up of three members; Magne Furuholmen, Paul Waaktaar-Savoy, and who?

3. How many UK number ones did Phyllis Nelson have?

4. Sister Sledge was made up of how many sisters?

5. How many UK number ones has Madonna had?

1. Vietnam 2. Morten Harket 3. 1 4. 4 5. 13

The 1980s was full of yummy treats and tasty desserts, just waiting for you to sticky your fingers with. Even school dinners came with a side of tasty cake – one in particular, was the jam & coconut sponge cake with pink custard, which is a favourite of many 80s kids!

Ingredients:

225g sunflower spread

225g caster sugar

225g self-raising flour

4 medium eggs

200g raspberry jam

25g desiccated coconut

500g custard

2 or 3 drops red food colouring

Method:

1. Heat the oven to 180 degrees and grease a rectangular cake tin then line with baking paper.

2. Put the sunflower spread, flour, sugar and eggs into a large bowl and mix well until smooth and creamy.

3. Pour the mixture into your cake tin, then pop it into the oven for 25-30 minutes. Then remove from the oven and allow to cool a little.

4. Put some jam into a bowl and stir until smooth, then spread evenly over the cake while still warm and sprinkle with coconut.

5. Mix the food colouring into the custard well, then heat through until hot.

6. Cut the sponge into squares, place into a bowl and pour some pink custard over the top.

Enjoy your blast to the past – and don't forget to blow your spoon first!

Nicknamed the 'Iron Lady', Margaret Thatcher was the longest standing prime minister in the 20th century. A member of the Conservative party, Thatcher ruled the government for the entirety of the 80s. Before becoming Prime Minister, Thatcher first worked as a research chemist, a barrister and then found her way as a member of parliament.

Test your knowledge of UK politics in the 80s here!

1. Margaret Thatcher won her first parliamentary election.

2. Margaret worked as a scientist developing soft scoop ice-cream.

3. Thatcher's family took in a Jewish girl before the Second World War.

4. Margaret Thatcher was married once before Denis Thatcher.

5. Margaret Thatcher was born in an apartment above her father's shop.

1. False – She lost her first two 2. True 3. True 4. False 5. True

Stay in the '80s
COAL NOT DOLE
VHS
JUST SAY NO!
Falkland Islands
West Falkland
East Falkland
STANLEY

80s architecture was focussed on bringing postmodernism to the scene! Contemporary square buildings became the in-thing, and concrete became an architect's best friend. Woodchip wallpaper was still high on the popularity list in the 80's for internal decor, and on the outside, roughcast was still a winner in finishing touches - with older buildings being replaced by blocky brutalism.

The 80s saw the erection of many iconic buildings around the world!

Here are some of the shining stars and record breakers:

Tower 42 - London

Known as the 'NatWest Tower', this skyscraper was completed in 1980, and was once the tallest building in the UK! With a construction cost of £72 million, it's a good job this building was once futuristic in style!

Ganter Bridge - Switzerland

Not a building but nonetheless iconic, the Ganter Bridge in Switzerland is the second longest bridge in the country, and shows greatly how concrete was used in many builds in the 80s. With a total length of 2,224 ft, this bridge is a whopper of a design!

Teresa Carreño Cultural Complex - Venezuela

Showing that the brutalist design spanned across the globe, this popular theatre in Venesuela is the second largest throughout South America. Named after the pianist Teresa Carreño, this venue covers an area of 860,000 square ft!

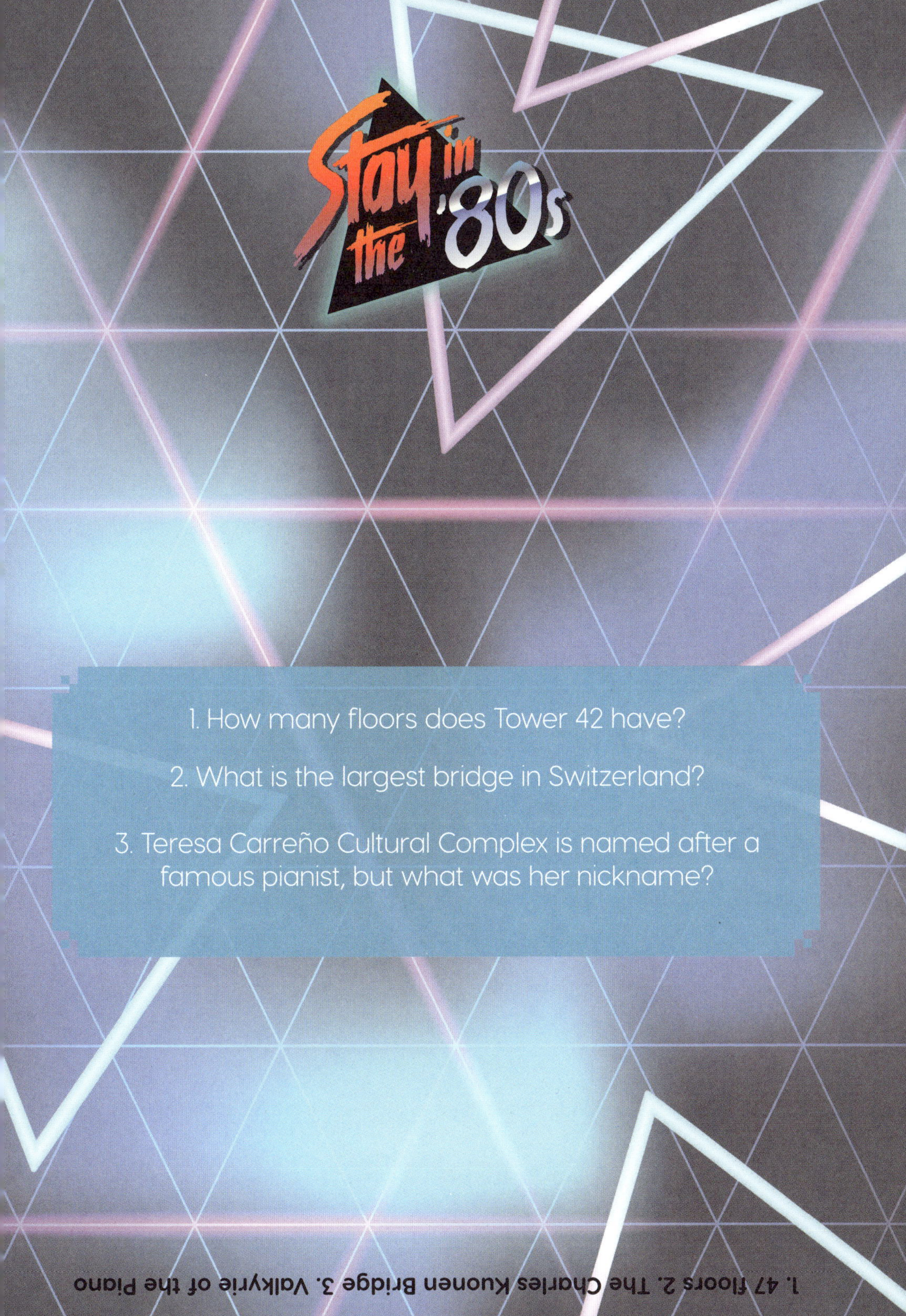
Stay in the '80s

1. How many floors does Tower 42 have?

2. What is the largest bridge in Switzerland?

3. Teresa Carreño Cultural Complex is named after a famous pianist, but what was her nickname?

1. 47 floors 2. The Charles Kuonen Bridge 3. Valkyrie of the Piano

Popular fashion in the 80s is still a defining feature of the decade, with many memories beginning in the clothes people wore! With some clothing and accessories still being a big hit in fashion today, let's take a trip down memory lane and remember some of the popular clothing trends from the 80s, some of which are still popular today!

Denim became a rising material in the 1980s, with people choosing casual denim jackets, jeans and even dungarees for everyday styles. Dungarees, as mentioned, were a staple in fashion for both men and women, and could be paired with a t-shirt or jumper, and boots or pumps.

Jazzy, vibrant fabrics were in! You could pair any two colours together and it would still be deemed socially acceptable. Neon zip-up jackets, stripy, baggy pants and shirts covered in squiggles are just some of the crazy finds in 80s fashion.

Fitness became big in the 1980s, with men donning a two piece tracksuit and vest in blues, greens and purples, while ladies sported vibrant leggings, leotards and legwarmers (to watch their VHS fitness classes!)

Shoulder pads made formalwear popular for both men and women, and could be found in most blazers and office dresses. Grey tartan could be spotted around offices and pubs after 5pm, and a neckerchief would often sit around a woman's neck.

Think you were a fashionista in the 80s?
See how much you really know!

1. Which jacket brand carried the slogan "When you put it on, something happens"?

2. Off-shoulder sweatshirts and legwarmers became a trending fashion in the 80s, but which movie inspired this look?

3. Which fabric accessory could you find many people wearing on their hands in the 80s?

4. The 'mom' is a style of what clothing which was popular in the '80s?

In 1986 – 21 singles hit number 1 in the UK charts, though there was a sure winner for biggest selling single that way – The Communards with Don't Leave Me This Way! This iconic 70's classic had a refresh with the duo's cover, their only number one ever, and they sold 768,500 copies in the one year.

The top 10 for 1986 in the UK was:

1. DON'T LEAVE ME THIS WAY - COMMUNARDS

2. EVERY LOSER WINS - NICK BERRY

3. I WANT TO WAKE UP WITH YOU - BORIS GARDINER

4. LIVING DOLL - CLIFF RICHARD & THE YOUNG ONES

5. CHAIN REACTION - DIANA ROSS

6. THE LADY IN RED - CHRIS DE BURGH

7. WHEN THE GOING GETS TOUGH, THE TOUGH GET GOING
- BILLY OCEAN

8. PAPA DON'T PREACH - MADONNA

9. TAKE MY BREATH AWAY - BERLIN

10. SO MACHO/CRUISIN - SINITTA

Test your knowledge of the 1986 UK charts with this quiz!

1. How many UK number ones did Berlin have?

2. In Sinitta's 'So Macho', what colour eyes should the man have?

3. Which all female group did Diana Ross find her fame as a member of?

4. Which album was Madonna's 'Papa Don't Preach' recorded for?

5. How many UK top tens did Billy Ocean have?

1. 12. Blue 3. The Supremes 4. True Blue 5. 6

The 80s is often seen as an in-between decade, with the 1970s inventing many pieces of tech and the 1990s making them more advanced like the tech we see around today. However, don't brush the 80s under the mat just yet, because this funky decade has its own claim to fame!

Weddings, christenings and children's birthdays were blessed with a cheap and cheerful piece of tech – disposable cameras! Take a look through your old photo album... how many of these reminiscent pics from your Aunt Jean's 40th birthday would have been taken on a cheap and tacky plastic Kodak?

If you took a day trip to Scarborough or hopped on a plane to some sandy beach, be assured that your mum would have about twenty of these cameras in her handbag, just waiting to be used, then rushed to a shop so the film can be developed. You'd have been told a thousand times not to let the film see the light of day, for fears that the many pictures of the sand would be ruined.

Take a shot of these snappy questions, to see if you developed your knowledge (or if you're running out of film)!

1. Which company is said to have brought out the first disposable camera in 1986?

2. Before this decade, a company called Photo-Pac brought out a similar concept – but which decade did this happen?
1930s/1940s/1950s/1960s

3. Which of these materials isn't used on disposable cameras?
Card/Plastic/Cotton/Metal

1. Fujifilm 2. 1940s 3. Cotton

Movie awards are a celebration of excellence and achievement in cinema, and are a great way to look at which films dominated this iconic decade!

The movie with the most awards in the 80s was Indiana Jones and the Raiders of the Lost Ark. This action-packed movie whipped up 11 awards in 1982, and is now considered one of the most successful adventure movies in history!

In 1981, The inspirational sports drama, Chariots of Fire won 3 awards, and then another 8 in 1982. These included BAFTA Awards for best film, best actor in a supporting role and best costume design, Academy Awards for best picture, writing, best music and more awards from the likes of the London Film Critic's Circle Award and the Golden Globe Award! – Talk about winning the race!

Some of the best actors and actresses got noticed in the 80s too! Meryl Streep won best actress award in 1983 for her role in 'Sophie's Choice', Robert De Nero won best actor in 1980 for his appearance in 'Raging Bull', and the very well-known Cher wound up winning best actress in the movie 'Moonstruck'!

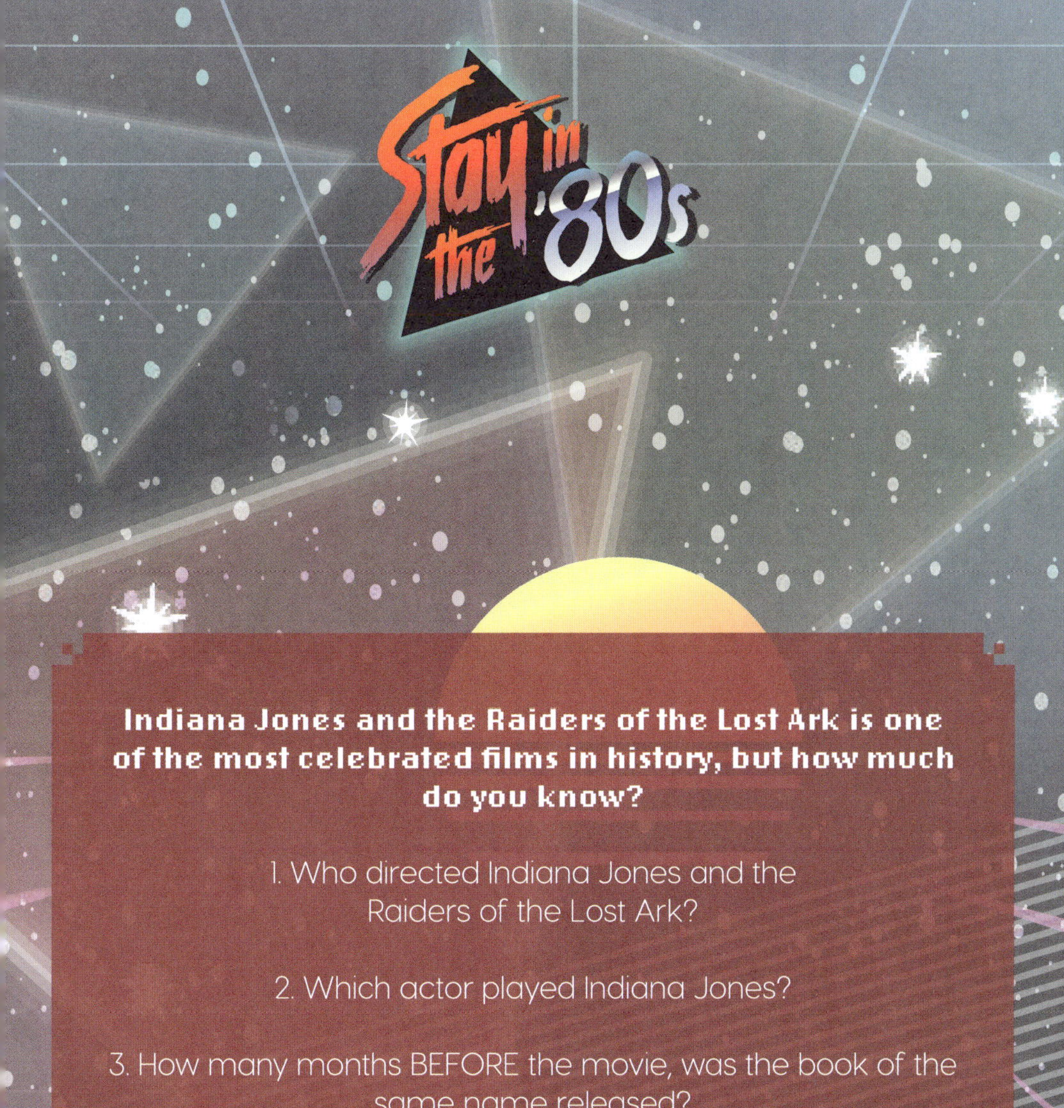

Indiana Jones and the Raiders of the Lost Ark is one of the most celebrated films in history, but how much do you know?

1. Who directed Indiana Jones and the Raiders of the Lost Ark?

2. Which actor played Indiana Jones?

3. How many months BEFORE the movie, was the book of the same name released?

4. Which animal phobia must Indiana conquer on his quest?

5. Which actress plays Indiana Jones' former lover?

1. Steven Spielberg 2. Harrison Ford 3. 2 months 4. Snake phobia 5. Karen Allen

80's

Whether you sported a rainbow coloured tracksuit, neon fishnets or monochrome stripes, this quick quiz should be easy for true children of the 80s!

1. In 'The Smurfs', who was the head villain?

2. Which pop duo released the song 'West End Girls'?

3. Madonna filed for divorce in 1987 from who?

4. Which artist released the album 'Thriller' in 1982?

5. When were CDs released to the public?

1. Gargamel 2. The Pet Shop Boys 3. Sean Penn 4. Michael Jackson 5. 1982

Name: Madonna (Madonna Louise Ciccone)
Born: August 16th , 1958
Occupations: Singer-songwriter and actress
Most Famous 80s Appearance: Taking to the stage to sing, in films including Desperately Seeking Susan

Madonna is a household name, and everybody knows somebody who was in awe of her musical talent and fashion. She took piano lessons as a child but convinced her father to allow her to take ballet lessons, as she wanted to become a dancer. Before fame, she worked at Dunkin' Doughnuts, and only became an icon in the early 80s.

How much do you know about this legendary Queen of Pop?

1. Madonna is also a children's book author.

2. Madonna has a massive fear of thunder.

3. Madonna has a star on the Hollywood Walk of Fame.

4. Madonna has 3 children.

5. Madonna's family own a vineyard in Michigan.

1. True 2. True 3. False 4. False – 4 5. True

When looking at CGI advancements in the 1980s, many much loved movies and TV shows made a stand. Let's take a look at just some films that made their screen time - BOOM!

Looker – 1981

This movie included the first use of 3D-shaded CGI and the first wholly computer generated human body!

Tron – 1982

This movie used 15 whole minutes of 3D CGI, which includes the iconic 'Light Cycle'!

The Last Starfighter – 1984

This movie is the first to use integrated CGI, which represent real-world objects!

Money For Nothing (Dire Straits) - 1985

Not a movie, but this is the first music video to be computer-generated!

Labyrinth – 1986

This iconic fantasy movie was the first to include a realistic CGI animal (the owl silly! Not David Bowie...)

Doctor Who (Season 24) – 1987

The first TV show to have a CGI opening sequence!

Indiana Jones and the Last Crusade - 1989

This adventure movie was the first movie to include an all-digital composite!

Stay in the '80s

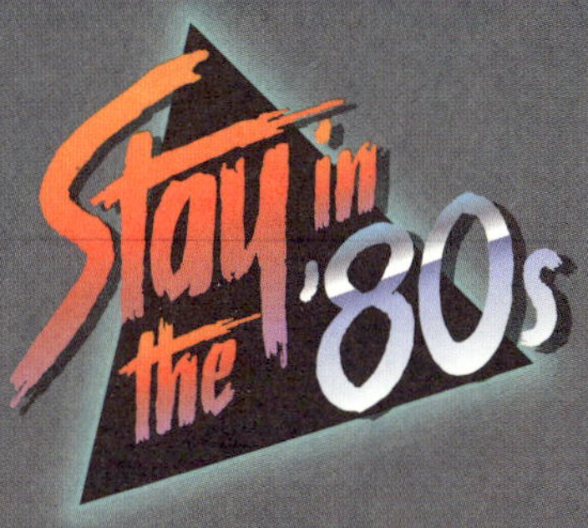

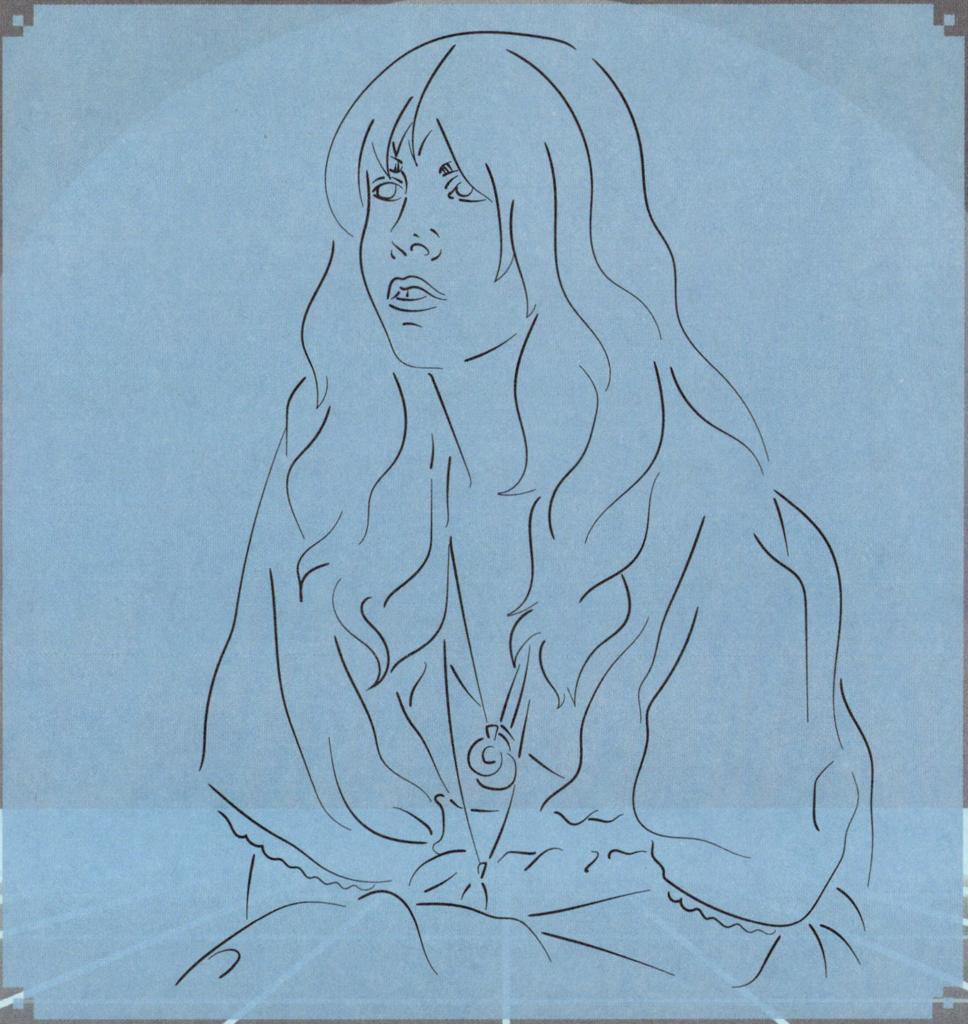

"It was my 16th birthday - my mom and dad gave me my Goya classical guitar that day. I sat down, wrote this song, and I just knew that that was the only thing I could ever really do - write songs and sing them to people."
- Stevie Nicks

Fingerless Gloves

One sure way to let people know you were an on-trend 80s kid was to never part with your fingerless gloves. You'd play out on the street, shower, eat your dinner and probably even sleep with these gloves on. Depending on your fashion calling, your gloves could either be woollen, neon netted or even leather – pick your poison!

Plastic Jewellery

The 80s wasn't the place for shiny gold or silver – plastic was the in-thing, baby! Chunky necklaces with beads the size of golf balls, large hoop earrings you could shoot your basketball through, and non-extendable neon bracelets you'd almost dislocate your wrists to wear... plastic was everywhere!

Fedoras

If you were a 'somebody' (and let's face it, all us 80s kids thought we were somebody), you would have owned this fancy bit of head attire. Everyone famous had one – Boy George, Debbie Gibson, Michael Jackson... who was your hat-wearing idol?

Test your knowledge of the must-have accessories of the 1980s – were you as cool as you think?

1. A slightly bent hairclip that pulled apart in the center, often used to hold ponytails... What was it called?

2. Which brand of sunglasses became a big thing in the 80s?

3. To add an iconic ruffle to the side of your t-shirt, you would probably buy what?

1. Banana clip 2. Ray Bans 3. T-shirt clip

If you grew up in the 1980s, then the likelihood is you had a yummy packed lunch. Not only that, they probably contained a lot more sugar and starch than you're even allowed to take these days...

In all likeliness, your parents would have hidden the gooey chocolate bars and pickled onion Space Raiders next to a sliced apple, Dairylea triangle and a handful of grapes...

If you had a biscuit bar, it was probably a Breakaway or Club, and you've probably tried dipping it into your fruity yogurt once or twice – yum!

You'd gleefully open your pack-up and poke your straw into a carton of orange juice (which lasted about one second), and look to see if you had any cookies or digestives to demolish before scoffing your sandwich.

And what was that filled with again? A block of cheese? Meat paste? Ham in the shape of a poor, helpless bear? Mothers really did try to outdo the other parents with their perfectly sliced bread and sweet treats!

1. What is the common name for a small pot of yogurt?

2. What was the name of everyone's favourite
bear-shaped ham?

3. The popular snack Wagon Wheels were invented
in what decade?

4. Name 3 flavours of Space Raider crisps (4 available).

1. Fromage Frais 2. Billy Bear
3. 1940s 4. Pickled Onion, Beef, Spicy, Saucy BBQ

The 1980s, like other decades, saw many new world records...

1. In 1980, Reinhold Messner from Italy, became the first solo climber to reach the top of Mount Everest. It took him three whole days from his camp at the base of the mountain, and didn't have any bottled oxygen as an aid!

2. Michael Jackson claims a world record in 1984, for best-selling album of all time (for now, wink, wink!). Thriller won 8 Grammy awards – including record and album of the year...

3. 1986 was shadowed by Bigfoot... No, not the hairy beast that hides in the woods... the world's largest monster truck! Bigfoot 5 was built by Bob Chandler in the USA. A massive 15 foot, 6 inches tall, this big beast weighs 17,236kg!

4. The very famous Richard Branson set his own record with his Swedish pilot Per Linstrand, as the duo crossed the Atlantic Ocean in a hot-air balloon, being the first people to do so! On 2nd July, 1987, the duo set off in Maine, USA and took just under 32 hours to reach the UK.

1. Sir Ranulph Fiennes and Charles Burton complete the first ever surface circumnavigation via both geographical poles in 1982. Which year did they begin this?

2. The first ever space shuttle flight was achieved in 1981 by NASA's shuttle. What was the shuttle called?

3. Roy Castle, the host of BBC's Record Breakers programme set a record of his own – what was it?

1. 1979 2. Columbia 3. Fastest time to perform one million taps!

Cars that were popular in the 1980s are often frowned upon in this day and age. There were no smooth curves or fancy gadgets, just great, well-built square machines that got you from A to B.

The most popular car of the 80s is quite obviously the Ford Escort, with a wheel-spinning 1,607,999 cars being registered throughout the 80s. There was quite a boom in the car market, as people relied on them more for travelling and commuting to work!

For the working man, the go to cars were the Ford Cortina, Vauxhall Astra and Nissan Micra. These cars were cheap and cheerful, and came in a range of square styles and colours.

If you were a bigger car enthusiast, you might have been tempted to go for a swanky new Chevy Camaro or Ferrari Testarossa, cars you only find now in vehicle museums or car collector's auctions!

See if you're a true petrol head with these fun questions on the most popular cars of the decade:

1. Which popular Ford car had wooden panels down the sides?

2. The movie 'Christine' was a horror film about a killer car of the same name... but what type of car was Christine?

3. Which Ford model shared its name with a type of horse?

4. What was Nissan's former name before their change in 1981?

5. The Bentley T-series began production in 1965 up until when?

1. Ford Station Wagon 2. 1958 Plymouth Fury 3. Ford Mustang 4. Datsun 5. 1980

What the UK public in 1987 didn't know is that they'd been rick-rolled! Yes, aiming for first in the UK charts of 87' was most certainly Rick Astley with his ever famous 'Never Gonna Give You Up'!

Now found at every milestone party, Mr Astley actually sold just over 766,000 copies in 87' alone! This iconic year was a breakthrough for Rick and his rolls, and he's stayed popular throughout the decades since!

The UK top 10 of 1987 looked like this:

1. NEVER GONNA GIVE YOU UP - RICK ASTLEY
2. NOTHING'S GONNA STOP US NOW - STARSHIP
3. I WANNA DANCE WITH SOMEBODY (WHO LOVES ME) - WHITNEY HOUSTON
4. YOU WIN AGAIN - BEE GEES
5. CHINA IN YOUR HAND - T'PAU
6. RESPECTABLE - MEL & KIM
7. STAND BY ME - BEN E KING
8. IT'S A SIN - PET SHOP BOYS
9. STAR TREKKIN' - FIRM
10. PUMP UP THE VOLUME - M/A/R/R/S

Think you know your music from 1987? Test yourself with this music-themed trivia!

1. In which county of the UK was Rick Astley born and raised?

2. What was the surname of both Mel and Kim?

3. What is the next word in Starship's 'Nothing's Gonna Stop Us Now' intro "Lookin' in your eyes, I see ......"?

4. Whitney Houston was the first woman of colour to appear on the cover of which magazine?

5. Rick Astley first started out as a drummer in a band. What was the band called?

1. Lancashire 2. Appleby 3. Paradise 4. Seventeen 5. FBI

The 1980s saw supermodels from a range of backgrounds and upbringings finally begin to get the representation they deserved on the runways!

Fashion houses such as Chanel, Oscar de la Renta and Christian Lacroix changed the face of fashion by diversifying their runways, adapting to modern times with bolder statements than ever before!

Big hair and even bigger shoulder pads were sported by the likes of Iman, Inès de La Fressange, Anna Bayle and Jerry Hall, amongst others!

How many do you recognise from the 80s?

Test your knowledge here:

1. Model Iman Famously married which British pop star?

2. Katoucha Niane became a muse to which 3-word French Fashion house?

3. Model-made-actress, Jerry Hall, starred in which 1989 film?

1. David Bowie 2. Yves Saint Laurent (YSL) 3. Batman

Test your decade knowledge with these fun 80s trivia questions. Remember, all of these are pot luck, so could be about any year and any topic – let's see how much of an 80s kid you really are!

Test your knowledge here:

1. Tainted Love was a hit for Soft Cell in 1981 - but who recorded the original?

2. The band A-ha originated from which country?

3. Singers Martha Wash and Izora Armstead are better known as who?

4. Prince Andrew married who in 1986?

5. In which year was Mark Zuckerberg born?

1. Gloria Jones 2. Norway 3. The Weather Girls 4. Sarah Ferguson 5. 1984

The 80s was the decade to be in if you needed entertaining. Movie fans were getting bored of the same old romance and cowboy movies, and wanted a little more fun and action in their lives.

Some franchises that began in the 80s still don our screens today. With iconic movies like Indiana Jones, Terminator, Die Hard and Ghostbusters still popping up on TV every Christmas, you can be assured that these movies will still be popular in 2080!

Would you consider Die Hard a Christmas movie?

Some of the best movie franchises of the 1980s include:

The Terminator
Indiana Jones
Back to the Future
Robocop
Die Hard

1. Which actor played the main role as Terminator in the movie franchise 'The Terminator'?

2. What is Robocop's human name?

3. What type of hat does Indiana Jones usually wear?

4. Which season of the year does Die Hard take place in?

5. In Back to the Future, what is Doc's full name?

1. Arnold Schwarzenegger 2. Alex Murphy 3. Fedora 4. Winter 5. Dr. Emmett Brown

The way people chose to decorate their homes in the 80s really did leave a dent in the styles of today. Much like the clothes people wore, the 1980s were mismatched and busy, but made us who we are.

Mahogany

This red-tinted wood really was the go-to when it came to wooden furniture. Bedside tables, coffee tables and TV stands, among others, could all be found in this cherry coloured material! (Let's face it, if your kitchen table didn't match your dresser, were you even an 80s kid?)

Tartan

Cushions, curtains and settees were often found in this traditional Scottish pattern. If you didn't feel like you travelled to the highlands when you crawled into bed at night or sat down to listen to the radio, then your family was probably the other kind of busy... florals!

Florals

Nothing made a room feel more homely than bringing the outdoors in. It didn't matter if none of the florals matched in colour or style, if it had flowers, it stayed! Yes, this is what the youth are reminded of whenever they visit their granny, but there's no bigger satisfaction than knowing your carpets match your drapes (literally!)

Mismatched colours and patterns

If you suffer from any kind of disorganisation phobia, look away now! An 80's home is something that can either fill you with joy, or plague you with nightmares. Colours of every colour, textiles that just don't make sense, and a home filled with ugly stripes and lilies... it's like walking into a circus funhouse – whilst drunk!

The 1980s saw many ground-breaking scientific discoveries and achievements, many of which we now take for granted and couldn't live without! Here are 5 examples of scientific events that made headlines throughout the decade!

1. Stealth planes were just a pigment of your imagination, until 1988, when the world's first radar-resistant aircraft, the F-117 Nighthawk, was brought to light. This plane was first tested in 1981, and was delivered to the US Air Force a year later.

2. In 1982, a successful heart transplant operation was performed, which helped to extend the life of a 61 year old cardiac patient, Barney Clark!

3. DNA fingerprinting wasn't a thing until the 80's. Accidentally discovered in 1984, Geneticist Alec Jeffreys came across this discovery while researching genetic markers. This is now used religiously by the police, scientists, and medical professionals!

4. The rings of Neptune were discovered in 1984, but the discovery was made definitive by the Voyager 2 spacecraft when it was flying past Neptune in 1989, taking photographs as it went!

5. A popular reason for the extinction of dinosaurs came about in 1989, when scientists found a link in the distinction to match the excess iridium found in the boundary layer on earth, which implied that the dinosaurs were struck by a massive meteor strike!

How much do you know about the scientific discoveries of the decade? Test your knowledge with these fun questions:

1. What is the Big Bang's scientific name?

2. What is said to rain on Neptune?

3. The gene responsible for cystic fibrosis was discovered in which year?

4. A bird species from New Zealand was included in an endangered species recovery plan in 1989, but what type of bird was this?

5. In 1983, the term computer 'virus' was introduced. Who introduced it?

1. The K-T extinction event 2. Diamonds 3. 1989 4. Kakapo 5. Fred Cohen

Another Christmas song to top the charts and haunt the radio like the ghost of Christmas past is Cliff Richard's Mistletoe and Wine! With four weeks at number one, Cliff's festive single had an estimated 737,000 sales in 1988!

The top 10 for 1988 in the UK was:

1. MISTLETOE & WINE - CLIFF RICHARD

2. THE ONLY WAY IS UP - YAZZ & THE PLASTIC POPULATION

3. I SHOULD BE SO LUCKY - KYLIE MINOGUE

4. ESPECIALLY FOR YOU - KYLIE MINOGUE & JASON DONOVAN

5. I THINK WE'RE ALONE NOW - TIFFANY

6. NOTHING'S GONNA CHANGE MY LOVE FOR YOU -GLENN MADEIROS

7. GROOVY KIND OF LOVE - PHIL COLLINS

8. HE AIN'T HEAVY, HE'S MY BROTHER - THE HOLLIES

9. WITH A LITTLE HELP FROM MY FRIENDS - WET WET WET/BILLY BRAGG

10. TEARDROPS - WOMACK & WOMACK

1. Is Kylie the older or younger sister of Dannii Minogue?

2. Who sung the original version of 'I Think We're Alone Now'?

3. How many UK number ones has the band The Hollies had?

4. What relation do Linda and Cecil Womack have to each other?

5. What is the first line of Kylie Minogue's 'I Should Be So Lucky'?

1. Older 2. Tommy James and the Shondells 3. 2
4. They're married 5. In my imagination

Another iconic lunchtime dessert at schools in the 80s, the cornflake tart put a smile on many children's faces growing up! Reminisce about your school days while baking some yourself!

Ingredients:

320g ready-rolled shortcrust pastry

A sprinkle of plain flour

50g butter

125g golden syrup

25g brown soft sugar

100g cornflakes

125g strawberry jam

Custard

Method:

1. Warm the oven to 180 degrees Celsius. Roll out the pastry onto a lightly floured surface, and use the rolling pin to gently place over a tart/cake tin, pressing the corners and sides down. Trim around the edges of pastry that hangs over the rim.

2. Line the pastry with baking paper, and fill with uncooked rice. Bake in the oven for 15 minutes, remove the rice and paper, then bake until golden brown
(around 5 minutes).

3. Heat up the butter, syrup and sugar in a small pan with a slight pinch of salt, and stir until melted and smooth. Put some cornflakes into the mixture, and mix until covered.

4. Spoon some jam into the pastry base, then tip the cornflake mix on top. Press down until all of the jam is covered. Pop into the oven for an extra 5 minutes.

5. Wait until the tart has cooled a little, and serve with custard.

Enjoy the tasty throwback!

80's

1. Mike Tyson became the youngest ever boxing Heavyweight Champion in 1986.

2. Michael Caine played Beetlejuice in the 1988 film of the same name.

3. Toothless Tommy was the name of the pirate captain in The Goonies.

4. The "Black Monday" stock market crash happened in 1987.

5. In 1981, the first woman travelled into space.

1. True 2. False – Michael Keaton 3. False – One Eyed Willy 4. True 5. False – 1963

6. In 1983, Thriller became the best-selling album of all time.

7. DNA fingerprinting was created in 1989.

8. DVDs were developed & released in 1985.

9. The lead singer of Blondie was Deborah Gibson.

10. Salt-N-Pepa consisted of 4 members.

6. True 7. False – 1984 8. False – 1997 9. False – Debbie Harry 10. False – 2

Much like any decade in history, the 1980s is home to some lesser-known, but wild, crazy and hilariously out-there facts and statistics that will really open your eyes!

1. In 1982, computer scientist Scott Fahlman blessed the world with emojis! Yes, he was the first person on earth to use a smiley emoticon!

2. Canada didn't have full independence from the UK until 1982, when Queen Elizabeth II authorised the Canada Act!

3. In 1987, 20% of all mattress sales in the world were for – you guessed it… WATERBEDS!

4. A not so cheerful fact, crack cocaine was first synthesised and produced in 1983 in the Bahamas, which soon spread across the globe.

5. It cost a whopping $20,000 to create the Stay Puft Marshmallow Man suit for the movie Ghostbusters, and the crew had to make three of them!

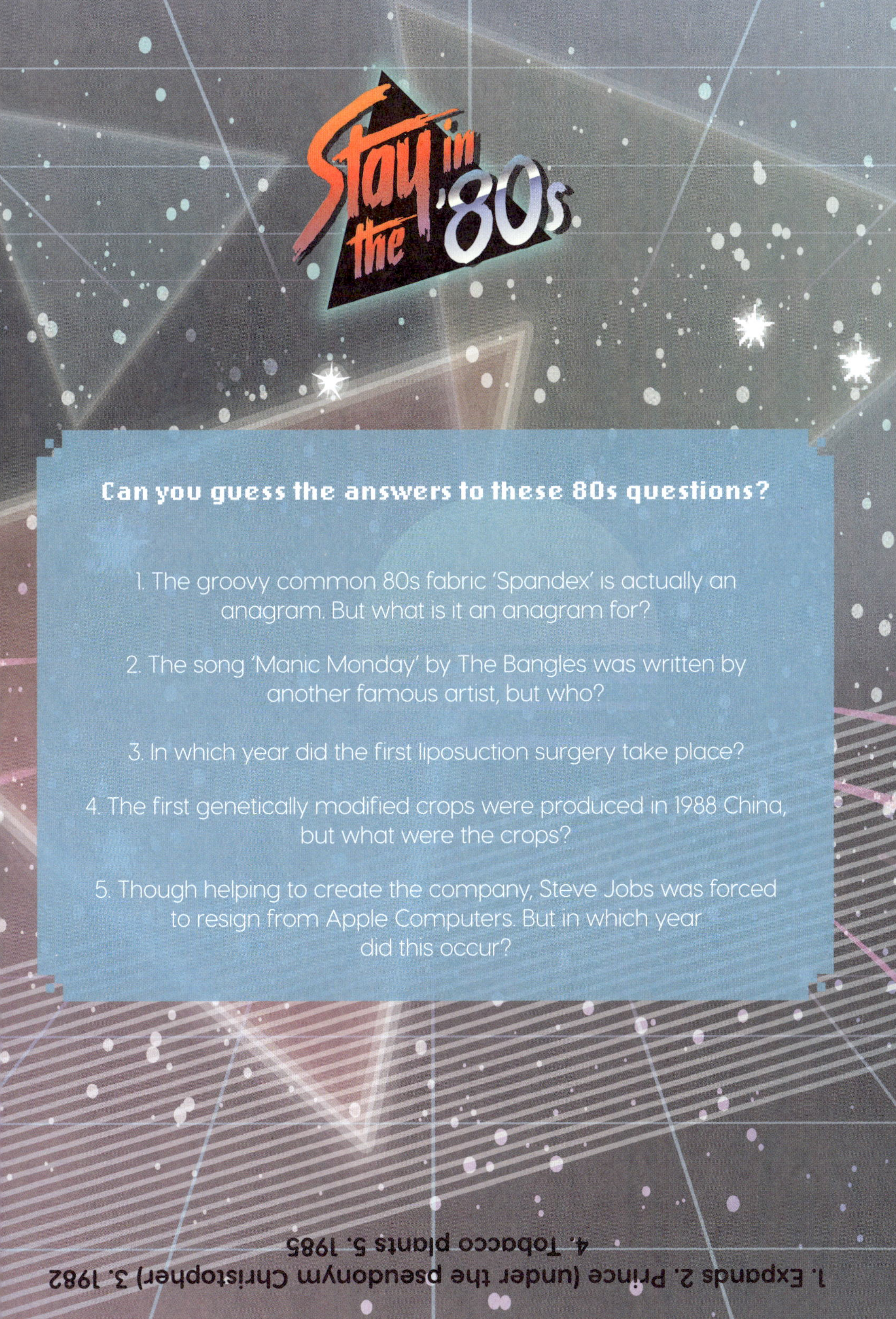

Stay in the '80s

Can you guess the answers to these 80s questions?

1. The groovy common 80s fabric 'Spandex' is actually an anagram. But what is it an anagram for?

2. The song 'Manic Monday' by The Bangles was written by another famous artist, but who?

3. In which year did the first liposuction surgery take place?

4. The first genetically modified crops were produced in 1988 China, but what were the crops?

5. Though helping to create the company, Steve Jobs was forced to resign from Apple Computers. But in which year did this occur?

1. Expands 2. Prince (under the pseudonym Christopher) 3. 1982 4. Tobacco plants 5. 1985

80'S
"We have powerful friends. You're going to regret this."
– Princess Leia from Star Wars: Return of the Jedi (1983)
played by Carrie Fisher

Think you know your telly? Test yourself with these questions!

1. In this most watched episode of EastEnders, Den Watts handed what item to Angie?

2. Prince Charles and Lady Diana Spencer married in 1981, but how old was Lady Spencer at this time?

3. In the TV series 'Dallas', what job did J.R. Ewing have?

4. Who Played Audrey Forbes-Hamilton in the 1980s episode of 'To the Manor Born'?

5. When did Coronation Street first air?

1. Divorce papers 2. 20 years old 3. Oil baron 4. Penelope Keith 5. 9th December 1960

There were many legendary movie quotes that came out in the 1980s, but how many of these do you know? See whether you know which film these quotes came from!

1. "I am serious. And don't call me Shirley."

2. "Don't mess with the bull young man, you'll get the horns."

3. "Snakes! Why'd it have to be snakes?"

4. "Wax on, wax off."

5. "Me, I always tell the truth, even when I lie! So, say good night to the bad guy!"

How many did you get right? What's your favourite movie quote of the decade?

1. Airplane! 2. The Breakfast Club 3. Raiders Of The Lost Ark 4. The Karate Kid 5. Scarface

Being a kid in the 80s, you'll most likely remember spending your pocket money on iconic sweets of the decade – some of which are still popular today!

Skittles, though first made commercially in the mid 70s, didn't become a big favourite of children until the 80s. These fruit flavoured sweets sure looked like a rainbow, and could take you on a trip with the amount of E numbers they contained.

The sticky, chewy sweet that is the Wham bar, was introduced to shop shelves in the early 80s. You could bet your last penny that you'd receive one of these as a treat – usually a little warm, bent and gooey!

Other popular sweets found in the pockets of school children were Drumstick lollies, Black Jacks, Parma Violets and Sherbet Fountains... YUM!

Kids of the 1980s loved sweets that were either sherbet filled, or left a sticky mess everywhere!

Do you have a sweet tooth? Let's find out!

1. Skittles are produced by the company Wrigley, but which confectionary company owns Wrigley?

2. A Sherbet Fountain had iconic yellow packaging and a sherbet filling, but what other sweet was found inside one?

3. What two colours is the 'WHAM' on an original Wham bar?

1. Mars, Inc 2. A liquorice stick 3. Red and yellow

80'S
back to 80's
"Carpe diem boys. Seize the day. Make your lives extraordinary!"
- John Keating, 'Dead Poets Society' (1989), played by Robin Williams

Movies in the 80s were all the rage, not only because of advancing technology, but for enhanced and unique props! Let's take a look at some props from popular 80s movies, and see where they are today!

Movie: A Christmas Story
Year: 1983

In this American Christmas comedy, there were legs – not just any legs though. No, these were leg lamps, and they were added onto everyone's letter to Santa on the year of the movie's release. Three original leg lamps were made for this movie, and while all were broken during production, knock-off legs soon became a big hit in households around the world. Enough legs sold that Christmas alone, that they could
reach the top of Everest!

Movie: Back to the Future Part II
Year: 1989

This iconic skateboard from the future was designed by toy company Mattel. This hoverboard became the new obsession of child fans – so Mattel did what they do best – created an iconic movie-themed toy! The original prop now resides in a private collection, but last sold at auction in 2018 for $42,500!

Movie: Big
Year: 1988

The movie Big was just that – big. If you've watched Big, you'll probably remember the iconic Zoltar machine, which many of us have seen at the seaside as a child. Nevertheless, this memorable prop only sold for a disappointing $8,500 in 2014... perhaps Zoltar wasn't playing nice!

80's
TOP GUN
Snakes. Why'd it have to be snakes?
Nothing in this game for two in a bed.
80's

Cassette tapes played a massive part in the development of music, but their time was over. Move along tapes, the CD has arrived!

In 1982, Sony released the first CD player available commercially, and called it the Sony CDP-101!

Dire straits released their album 'Brothers in Arms' in 1985, and unbelievably to most, the CD actually outsold the cassette, a breakthrough in the music industry. CD sales soon rose, and they became a more permanent feature – with more and more artists pushing the cassette aside to make way for the new generation.

Portable CD players soon hit the market, changing the way we listen to music – forever!

What did you use to listen to music in the 1980s?

80'S
Here's Jonny
PRESS START

One of the most famous and recognisable artists of the 1980s was Jean-Michel Basquiat. Basquiat's 'Untitled', painted in 1982, is one of his most famous and recognisable paintings, showing a skull over a blue graffiti-style background.

Born in New York, Basquiat began as a graffiti artist, before shooting to fame in the 1980s! Untitled shows a turning point in his career, and is still one of the most expensive paintings ever sold, selling for $110.5 million in 2017!

How much do you know about Jean-Michel Basquiat? Test your knowledge here:

1. Which famous Pop Artist became extremely close friends with Basquiat in the 1980s?

2. Which genre of art is Basquiat's work generally classified as?
A) Fauvism, B) Pop Art, C) Abstract Expressionism, D) Neo-Expressionism

3. In which decade did Basquiat die of a drug overdose?

1. Andy Warhol 2. Neo-expressionism 3. 1980s

Leading the charts for six weeks, Black Box rose to the top with their hit "Ride On Time". With 849,000 sales for 1989, this dance hit had people moving onto the dancefloor at every club or party!

The top 10 for 1989 in the UK was:

1. RIDE ON TIME - BLACK BOX

2. SWING THE MOOD - JIVE BUNNY & THE MASTERMIXERS

3. ETERNAL FLAME – THE BANGLES

4. TOO MANY BROKEN HEARTS - JASON DONOVAN

5. BACK TO LIFE - SOUL II SOUL FT. CARON WHEELER

6. SOMETHING'S GOTTEN HOLD OF MY HEART - MARC ALMOND FT GENE PITNEY

7. THAT'S WHAT I LIKE - JIVE BUNNY & THE MASTERMIXERS

8. PUMP UP THE JAM - TECHNOTRONIC FT FELLY

9. DO THEY KNOW IT'S CHRISTMAS? - BAND AID

10. HAND ON YOUR HEART - KYLIE MINOGUE

Test your knowledge of the 1989 UK charts by answering these 5 questions!

1. Which country are Black Box from?

2. In which soap opera did Jason Donovan originally achieve his fame?

3. The Bangles only reached UK number one once. How long did they stay at the peak?

4. What is the first line of Kylie's 'Hand On Your Heart'?

5. How many UK number ones has Jive Bunny & The Mastermixers had?

1. Italy 2. Neighbours 3. 4 weeks 4. Put your hand on your heart and tell me 5. 3

80's

One of the most defining artists of the 80s was Keith Haring. His distinctive pop-art style paintings were inspired by the graffiti culture in New York City, and his use of bright colours and fun, cartoon-style figures was a hit amongst both art fans, and the general public!

His designs began to appear all over, in the form of posters, albums, clothing and interior design, quickly making him one of the most influential and popular modern artists ever – his designs are still popular today!

Test your knowledge with this fun true or false quiz:

1. Keith Haring was born in New Jersey.

2. One of Keith Haring's paintings sold for over $6 million dollars in 2017.

3. All 3 of Keith Haring's siblings had a first name beginning with 'K'.

4. Keith Haring died in 1990.

5. He famously hated Madonna in the late 1980s.

1. False - Pennsylvania 2. True 3. True 4. True 5. False - They were close friends.

In 1985, in Mexico City, amateurs stole over 120 artefacts from the National Museum of Archaeology. Sounds like a pretty standard heist, right? What makes this surprising is that the two culprits were not criminal masterminds or government officials, but largely talentless college dropouts!

All it took was some scoping around the museum, including a map of the air vents, and a lot of delusion! Now hailed as one of Mexico's greatest art heists, the goods were eventually discovered and the two culprits, Carlos Perches Trevino and Ramon Sardina Garcia were arrested!

Take a stab at these fun questions about the infamous theft!

1. Many of the items taken were considered priceless, but there was one particular vase that was valued pre-heist at how many millions of dollars?

2. True or False – This heist was recreated through a Mexican television series.

3. What were the guards doing on Christmas Eve in 1985 that allowed for the heist to happen?
A) They were away, B) They were trapped, C) They were drunk

1. 20 2. FALSE – It was recreated through a film in 2018 called Museo. 3. C) They were drunk

"Dear Diary, my teen-angst bullsh*t now has a body count."
– Veronica Sawyer from Heathers (1988) played by Winona Ryder

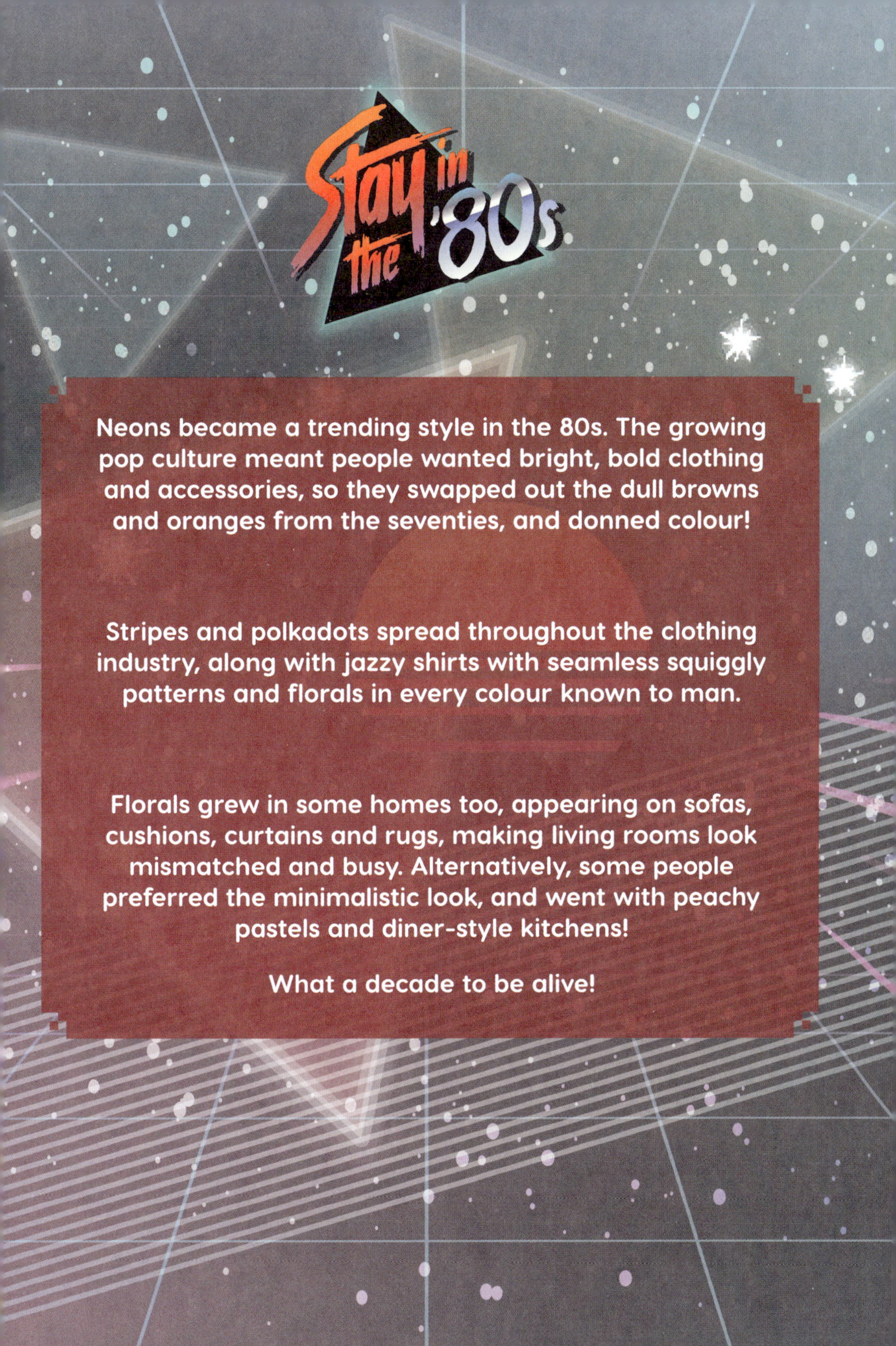

Neons became a trending style in the 80s. The growing pop culture meant people wanted bright, bold clothing and accessories, so they swapped out the dull browns and oranges from the seventies, and donned colour!

Stripes and polkadots spread throughout the clothing industry, along with jazzy shirts with seamless squiggly patterns and florals in every colour known to man.

Florals grew in some homes too, appearing on sofas, cushions, curtains and rugs, making living rooms look mismatched and busy. Alternatively, some people preferred the minimalistic look, and went with peachy pastels and diner-style kitchens!

What a decade to be alive!

80's

Bookworms of the 1980s were certainly treated with some awesome reads! From timeless action books to legendary and ground-breaking science and non-fiction publications, the 1980s will go down in history as a game-changer in terms of literature! Here are a few of the most iconic books that were published in the 1980s!

In 1980, Robert Ludlum released Bourne Identity – the start of a long series of books that tells the story of Jason Bourne, an action man with retrograde amnesia, who is on the search for his true identity. This book would be the first of a whopping 22 books!

In 1988, Stephen Hawking released his historic Cosmological book, A Brief History of Time. Intended to be read by people with little to no prior knowledge of physics, this book was ground-breaking in opening up the cosmological and physical discussion of space and time to the normal person, and is bound to have inspired many physicists of today!

In 1982, Alice Walker released the legendary fiction novel, The Colour Purple. About the traumas and successes of the central character, Celie, this book had immediate critical acclaim, receiving the National Book Award for Fiction!

How much do you know about the bestsellers of the 80s?

1. Who acted as Jason Bourne in the 2002 film adaption?

2. Who directed the 1985 film adaption of The Colour Purple?

3. How many books did Stephen King publish in the 1980s?
A) 11, B) 16, C) 22

4. Published in 1985, what was the name of Margaret Atwood's dystopian novel?

5. Roald Dahl published which book in 1988 that features characters such as The Wormwoods, Amanda Thripp and Hortenesia?

1. Matt Damon 2. Stephen Spielberg 3. B) 16 4. The Handmaid's Tale 5. Matilda

If you find yourself feeling like you're trapped on a desert island on a sunny day, don't panic! This refreshing cocktail, that shares its name with the 1980's survival drama movie, Blue Lagoon, is sure to leave you feeling refreshed!

Ingredients:

Ice

Orange slice

30ml Vodka

30ml Blue Curacao

20ml Lime Juice
Topped with lemonade

Tools:

Your favourite 80s glass (should be slim and tall)

A straw to sip from

Cocktail umbrella – you know you want to!

Method:

Pour the vodka, curacao and lime juice into a glass
and stir well.

Fill up the glass with ice and fill to the
top with lemonade.

Set out your sun lounger and relax in an
80s tropical paradise!

Comedy in the 1980s was hugely important, carving out a path for television comedians and programmes for years to come – some may call it a defining decade for the sitcom format of which we know and love today!

One of the decade's most popular comedy shows – Blackadder – first aired on BBC One on 15th June 1983, and consisted of four separate historical themes! Starring Rowan Atkinson, Hugh Laurie and Stephen Fry, Blackadder's dry humour was to define British Humour in its own right, which can be seen to be replicated in future comedies such as Father Ted and The Office.

In 1982, The Young ones came to our screens, following four very different students! This comedic bunch brought along cheeky, anarchic humour to households across the country, and is still referenced by many today!

Just like all British humour, Hi-de-Hi was a favourite to many! Set in 1959, this comedy series began in 1980 and was set in a holiday camp based in Essex. Starring comedy icons such as Su Pollard, David Griffin and Paul Shane, it's no wonder it lasted a whole 8 years!

Only Fools and Horses is probably the peak of British comedy. The show overlooks brotherly duo, Del Boy and Rodney Trotter, through their business blunders while dealing with funny problems and trying to become millionaires. Even today's generation will know this show, as all 64 episodes are often re-run on daytime TV!

Think your knowledge of comedy is gold?
Why not test yourself!

1. What is the name of the pub most commonly shown in 'Only Fools and Horses'?

2. Who played Spike Dixon in 'Hi-de-Hi'?

3. How many episodes of 'The Young Ones' were aired?

4. Which period was 'Blackadder Goes Forth' set?

1. The Nags Head 2. Jeffrey Holland 3. 12 4. 1917, First World War

"You ought to spend a little more time trying to make something of yourself
and a little less time trying to impress people."
- Vernon, The Breakfast Club (1985) played by Paul Gleason

The eighties was notorious for wild hairstyles. If your head was plagued with frizz, then you were probably the most popular kid at school.

Mullets were the 'in thing' no matter your gender. Long silky locks at the sides, pineapple prickles on top – and an absolute bonus if your mum cut it for you!

And then there were Jheri curls. These bouncy springs of hair took hours to achieve if you weren't born with the right hair type, and if you didn't touch up with a can of hairspray at least once an hour, then it was bound to fall flat by 11am.

People began to experiment with unnatural colours – bright red, orange, blue, green... They became walking rainbows (especially if they had a Mohawk!)

As is the case in nearly every decade in history since the modern Olympic games began, the 1980s was home to its own fair share of records, controversies and history-changing events!

Home to three Summer Olympic games (1980, 1984 and 1988), and three further Winter Olympic games hosted in the same years, let's take a look back and test your knowledge of the most memorable moments!

From boycotting and cheating, to record-breaking medals and achievements, the 80s Olympics have certainly gone down in history!

1. What did 65 countries refuse to do at the 1980 Olympic Games in Moscow?

2. In which Asian City were the 1988 Summer Olympic Games held?

3. Ben Johnson was famously stripped of his gold medals, and his world record, due to failing to pass a drug test. However, which athletics event did he compete in?

4. Which famous British ski jumper came last in both the 70 meter and 90 meter ski jump events at the 1988 Winter Olympics in Calgary, Canada?

5. Which iconic ice skating duo won in Ice dancing with perfect scores in 1984?

1. Refuse to play (Boycott) 2. Seoul 3. 100m sprint 4. Eddie the Eagle 5. Torvill and Dean

Dogs are a must-have pet for many families, and the same could be said for households in the 1980s! Here are just some of the trending dog breeds from this decade!

The cocker spaniel was one of the top-trending dog breeds from the 80s, but this wasn't always the case. After the 1950s dog-loving movie, Lady and the Tramp, spaniel sales boomed, but soon the popularity of this dainty dog spiralled down.

Labradors also rose to popularity, with advancements on training them up as service dogs, as well as their soft, and child-friendly nature – who wouldn't want a labrador pup?!

Whether it's the curly locks that represent the 80s hairstyle trends, or their intelligence, one thing's for certain, the poodle became one of the much-loved dogs of the decade!

Did you own a dog growing up? If so, was it one of the more popular breeds listed above?

Are you a true canine lover? See how much you know about the most popular, and famous, dogs of the 1980s!

1. What breed of dog was Beethoven, in the movie of the same name?

2. What was the name of Doc's pooch in Back to the Future?

3. What breed of dog was Comet from the TV series Full House?

4. What is the name of Scooby Doo's nephew?

5. What was the name of Sarah's dog companion in the fantasy movie, Labyrinth?

1. Longhaired St. Bernard 2. Einstein 3. Golden Retriever 4. Scrappy Doo 5. Ambrosius

The 1980s saw many household names enter the world; actresses, TV stars, singers, and sports personalities!

Celebrities born in this decade are now in their 30s and 40s, so most of the biggest stars that emerged from the 80s found fame through acting and singing – a change in some of the newer internet stars that were born in the 90s!

Let's take a look at which stars were born in the eighties:

1980 – Kim Kardashian, Macaulay Culkin, Venus Williams, Christina Aguilera

1981 – Beyoncé Knowles, Meghan Markle, Roger Federer, Britney Spears

1982 – Anne Hathaway, Kate Middleton, Lil Wayne, Nicki Minaj

1983 – Chris Hemsworth, Amy Winehouse, Emily Blunt, Jonah Hill

1984 – Scarlett Johansson, Mark Zuckerberg, Prince Harry, LeBron James

1985 – Christiano Ronaldo, Michael Phelps, Gal Gadot, Kiera Knightley

1986 – Lady Gaga, Usain Bolt, Emilia Clarke, Drake

1987 – Lionel Messi, Elliot Page, Blake Lively, Zac Efron

1988 – Conor McGregor, Adele, Rihanna, Rupert Grint

1989 – Taylor Swift, Daniel Radcliffe, Brie Larson, Anthony Joshua

How many of these names do you recognise?
Test your knowledge here:

1. Before marrying Prince Harry, Meghan Markle acted in which long-running US TV drama?

2. How many studio albums did Amy Winehouse release, prior to her tragic passing in 2011?

3. Which girl group was Beyoncé in, before beginning her solo career?

4. At which UK university did Kate Middleton meet Prince William?

5. What was the first Premier League club that Christiano Ronaldo played for?

1. Suits 2. 2 (Frank, Back to Black) 3. Destiny's Child 4. St Andrews 5. Manchester United

Can you guess how much items used to cost back in 1980, if you are given the cost of them thirty years later, in 2020? Some might surprise you – are we paying less, or more?

Test yourself with this fun and challenging quiz!

1. If in 2020, a First Class stamp cost 76p, how much did it cost in 1980?

2. If, in 2020, a Wall's Viennetta cost approximately £1.79, how much did it cost on its introduction in 1982?

3. If, in 2020, a loaf of bread cost £1.05, how much did it cost in 1980?

4. If the average property price in 2020 was £234,000, how much was it in 1980?

5. If the average cost of a car in 2020 is around £24,000, how much was it in 1980?

1. 12p 2. 72p 3. 39p 4. £23,287 5. £4,200

Stay in the '80s

Why not have a laugh with the other 80s babies you know with these jokes!

What do you call a spider that likes 80s music?
A Durantula.

What would happen if Whoopi Goldberg married Scooby-Doo?
Whoopi Doo!

What's the name of Mr. T's girlfriend?
April, fools!

People think that just because I grew up back in the 80s, I should walk around carrying a big ol' boom box on my shoulder.
But I refuse to go with that stereotype.

An 80s singer caught himself on fire, what does he do?
Stop, Drop, and Rick-Roll.

Who says 80s kids don't have a sense of humour?! Prove them wrong with these hysterical one-liners!

My wife keeps telling me to stop singing
"Stand and Deliver" every day.
I refused. I was Adam Ant.

How many Metalheads does it take to screw in a light bulb?
100. 1 to screw it in, and 99 to tell you that light bulbs were better in the 80s.

A man with a gun barged into the pub earlier and was threatening violence if the bar didn't play some classic 80s tunes.
Luckily The Police turned up and sorted him out.

For the first time ever I understood what all the fuss about 80s music was...
It was an A-ha moment!

How long did Lionel Richie sit on the toilet?
All night Long!

Reminisce in the best decade ever with these hilarious 80s jokes!

What's another term for a warm 80s drink?
Mr. Tea

What do you call an 80s band comprising of only fruit?
Durian Durian!

What's the Queen's favourite Prince song?
Purple Reign!

Why would someone want to have a DeLorean as a second car?
They could drive it from time to time!

What did Darth Vader say when the record store employee told him they were out of George Michael albums?
"I find your lack of 'Faith' disturbing."

What did Arnold Schwarzenegger say when he was invited to a classical composers costume party?
"I'll be Bach!"

What's wrong with Bonnie Tyler's GPS?
It keeps telling her to turn around, and every now and then it falls apart!

Why did the '80s kid always put the Christmas manger scene in the middle of the room?
Nobody puts Baby in the corner!

Which film won't Rick Astley let you borrow from his Pixar collection?
He's never going to give you Up!

Just like hairdos that were popular amongst women of the world, male hairstyle trends also changed drastically in the 1980s, and some have even come back into fashion recently, showing that they really have stood the test of time!

How many of these hairdos do you remember?

The mullet is a style which really does stand the test of time... this long at the back, choppy at the front look really was a popular choice for men who wanted a little length with their locks!

Perms also popped into fashion for men, giving an added bit of flair to the already wacky fashion statements – either that or 80's men just loved to eat their crusts!

If you wanted to woo a lady, you might instead opt for the slicked back look. All you needed was a fine toothed comb and a full jar of hair gel to get your hair looking soaking wet!

Try your knowledge of some retro dos!

1. Which popular 80s hairstyle is described as being 'business in the front, party in the back'?

2. A rock band who just so happened to have bushy hair in the 80s fell into which specific genre?

3. The popular 80s hairstyle, the Jheri Curl, was invented by who?

1. Mullet 2. Hair Metal 3. Jheri Redding – A hairdresser

The 1980s saw many iconic horror films released, that have now established themselves as cult classics! Which was your favourite horror film from the 80s?

The birth of legendary film series such as Gremlins, Friday the 13th and A Nightmare on Elm Street all occurred in the 80s and other cult classics such as The Shining, Hellraiser and The Evil Dead also terrified audiences around the world!

How much do you know about the legendary horror movies of the 1980s?

1. What was the monster called in A Nightmare on Elm Street?

2. Who was the actress who played Wendy in The Shining?

3. Which 1986 horror film famously features Jeff Goldblum?

4. Which Hollywood A-Lister stars as Adam in Tim Burton's Beetlejuice?

5. What type of creature features in The Lost Boys?

1. Freddie Kreuger 2. Shelley Duvall 3. The Fly 4. Alec Baldwin 5. Vampires

We all know a friend or family member who believes that Bigfoot and the Loch Ness Monster are in league with each other.

Whether they're just imaginative, or have a few screws missing, it's no lie that conspiracy theories have dominated history, and with every great event, there is usually multiple conspiracy theories that accompany it!

Let's take a look back at some of the major conspiracy theories that were born in the 1980s!

What caused the Chernobyl nuclear disaster

This terrible 80s nuclear disaster has its own share of theories into what actually happened.

Instead of believing the government and news stations, some people opted to listen to rumours... that aliens caused it. Or the CIA.

Or even that it was all a test to see what happens when things are affected by radiation. Not only that, but some people to this day even believe that the whole thing was a hoax.

Crop Circles

If aliens causing a nuclear disaster wasn't wacky enough, then maybe them visiting Earth just to draw circles in our crops is!

In the late 80s, crop circles and the theories behind them began to boom. How did these magnificent cuttings that resembled circles, runes and other shapes appear overnight, with nobody noticing?

How well can you answer these conspiracy themed questions?

1. Which curse is said to have played a part in the demise of the sinking of the Titanic?

2. What is the name of the racehorse which was allegedly taken at gunpoint in 1983?

3. Milk, vodka and even cucumbers were alleged to do what after the Chernobyl nuclear disaster?

1. Mummy's Curse 2. Shergar 3. Cure radiation poisoning

You either loved him or hated him, but one thing's for certain...
if you were a kid growing up in the 80s, you're sure
to remember him.

He-Man!

To some, he was just a character on a screen, but to others, he was
a hero! A strong, masculine idol for all young boys to look up to.
First airing in 1983, He-Man and the Masters of the Universe is the
first cartoon to be made solely to increase sales of toys! With two
years of running, and starring in 130 episodes, it's no wonder fans
and avid collectors are still around today!

Think you know your Masters of the Universe episodes? Why not test yourself!

1. What planet is Queen Marlena from?

2. Underneath her helmet, what colour is Evil-Lyn's hair?

3. Which toy company owned and produced the toys for
"Masters of the Universe"?

4. Who is She-Ra to He-Man?
Love interest / Daughter / Sister / Cousin

5. What is He-Man otherwise known as?

1. Earth 2. White 3. Mattel 4. She-Ra is He-Man's twin sister!
5. Prince Adam Glenn Grayskull

"Haven't you ever heard of the healing power of laughter?" –The Joker from Batman (1989) played by Jack Nicholson

The 1980s was when many popular theatre franchises that we know and love today, began!

Audiences from all over the world were fascinated with the glitz and glamour of Broadway and the West End, and some of Theatre's greatest stars who are known worldwide today, began performing in smaller-scale productions in the 80s!

One of the most popular and iconic stage productions of the 20th and 21st centuries is Andrew Lloyd Webber's Cats.

First performed on the 11th May 1981, Cats was inspired by a 1939 poetry collection by T.S. Eliot, called 'Old Possum's Book of Practical Cats', and between London and New York, has since been performed over 16,000 times!

How much do you know about Cats? Test your knowledge with these fun questions!

1. Which actress famously played the role of Grizabella in the original production of Cats?

2. In which year was a film production of Cats released, that starred celebrities such as Taylor Swift, James Corden and Jennifer Hudson?

3. In which city has Cats been performed more – London or New York?

4. Which famous song from Cats ends with the lyrics: 'If you touch me, you'll understand what happiness is ... Look, a new day has begun'?

5. What were the tribe of cats called in this musical?

1. Elaine Paige 2. 2019 3. London 4. Memory 5. The Jellicles

Having already covered the best-selling singles of each year, we have yet to look into the albums: what were the most successful albums of the 80s? With cassettes – and records – still being very popular, and CDs finally beginning to come into their own in this decade, the way in which people listened to their albums changed massively in the 80s!

Dire Straits had the best-selling album of the 1980s in the UK with Brothers in Arms, which surprisingly beat both Michael Jackson's Bad and Thriller! Released on the 17th May 1985, it spent a total of 14 weeks at the top spot on the UK albums chart, and has since sold over 30 million copies worldwide! It was also one of the first albums that was predominantly marketed towards the CD market, which could be one of the reasons for its success!

The top 10 biggest selling albums of the decade were:

1. BROTHERS IN ARMS – DIRE STRAITS

2. BAD – MICHAEL JACKSON

3. THRILLER – MICHAEL JACKSON

4. GREATEST HITS – QUEEN

5. KYLIE – KYLIE MINOGUE

6. WHITNEY – WHITNEY HOUSTON

7. TANGO IN THE NIGHT – FLEETWOOD MAC

8. NO JACKET REQUIRED – PHIL COLLINS

9. THE JOSHUA TREE – U2

10. TRUE BLUE – MADONNA

How much do you know about the biggest selling albums of the eighties, and the artists who released them?

1. In which country were Dire Straits formed?

2. What's the opening line to Michael Jackson's song, Thriller?

3. Which Fleetwood Mac song, that is third on the track listing for Tango in the Night, features the lyric 'Can you hear me calling out your name?'

4. Which band was Phil Collins famously a member of, before embarking on his solo career?

5. In which major Australian city was Kylie Minogue born?

1. England 2. It's close to midnight 3. Everywhere 4. Genesis 5. Melbourne

The 1980s was full of celebrity scandals, from lip-syncing fails to drugs charges – how many tabloid page-turners can you remember from the 80s? Here are two of the most iconic to jog your memory!

Lip Sync Assassins

Now largely forgotten, pop duo Milli Vanilli were rising stars in the 1980s! A German/French group hailing from Munich, Milli Vanilli's debut album, Girl You Know It's True went platinum a whopping 6 times, earning them a Grammy Award for Best New Artist!

However, during a performance on MTV in 1989, their success came crashing down. Their backing track skipped, revealing to the world that they were in fact… lip syncing! This scandal blew up, leading to the withdrawal of their Grammy and essentially ending their careers!

Ferris Bueller's Car Crash

In the 1980s, stars didn't get much bigger than Matthew Broderick. Main actor of Ferris Bueller's Day Off, Broderick was a much loved heartthrob of the decade! After the film, him and his on-screen sister, Jennifer Grey, began a real-life romance!

On a couple's retreat to Northern Ireland, Broderick was driving Grey during a bout of bad weather, during which he slid into the wrong lane and collided head on with a Volvo, killing both the driver and her passenger! Broderick was given a sentence of death by dangerous driving, but only wound up paying a $175 fine – scandalous!

How much do you know about other celeb scandals of the 1980s? Test your knowledge with these 5 fun questions:

1. The Vatican famously condemned which 80s pop music video?

2. Ozzy Osbourne bit the head off of which animal during a live show in 1982?

3. Paul McCartney was arrested in Japan at customs for what?

4. Which famous R&B/Soul singer was murdered by his father in 1984?

5. What are preachers such as Jim Bakker and Billy Graham called, who became famous through televised sermons?

1. Like A Prayer – Madonna 2. A bat 3. Smuggling in marijuana 4. Marvin Gaye 5. Televangelists